FROM THE HEART OF A BEAR

*True Stories of the Faith and Courage of
Children Facing Life-Threatening Illnesses*

JoAnn Zimmerman

Lazarus
Publishing
Des Moines, IA

FROM THE HEART OF A BEAR
True Stories of the Faith and Courage of
Children Facing Life-Threatening Illnesses

JoAnn Zimmerman

Published by:
Lazarus Publishing
P.O. Box 3525
Des Moines, IA 50323-3525

Printed in Canada

Hignell Book Printing,
Winnipeg, Canada

Copyright © 2005 by JoAnn Zimmerman
Library of Congress Control Number: 2005904087
ISBN 0-9769392-0-7

FROM THE HEART OF A BEAR

True Stories of the Faith and Courage of
Children Facing Life-Threatening Illnesses

JoAnn Zimmerman

Lazarus
Publishing
Des Moines, IA

Table of Contents

Acknowledgements

I thank
my God
who gave me a love for children,
a compassionate heart,
and a listening spirit,
and who blesses me moment by moment.

I thank
all the children and families who welcomed me
into their homes and hearts
and all the grieving families
whose tears and pain
have touched me deeply and will never be forgotten.

I thank
Lisa Flyr, my daughter,
and Bill Sheridan
a dear and faithful friend,
both of whom set loving, careful, often tired eyes
on the many drafts of all the revisions,
giving candid, clear, and respectful feedback.

I thank
G. Ray Bushyager
whose photographs appear throughout
this book. His generosity and commitment
to taking all the camp photographs is deeply appreciated.

I thank
Margaret Zimmer
who has volunteered tirelessly on so many projects
and has given her all when I needed her most.
Her quiet manner, positive outlook, and willing spirit
have made her a joy to work with and a treasured friend.

I thank
Gene Merz, S.J.
who has encouraged the writing of this book
from the very beginning.
His friendship, unending support, and
belief in me is a gift and a grace in my life.

I thank
Creighton University Retreat Center
and their caring staff
who always made me feel welcome
and provided me a prayerful, peaceful setting
where I could write, pray, and reflect,
and where my dog, Ashlin, was as welcome as I.

I thank
all the caring donors to Amanda the Panda
whose faithful monetary contributions – large or small -
made it possible to never charge a penny to any family
for our services for the past 25 years.

I thank
all the many volunteers who staff the camp,
wrap the gifts, prepare the meals for our support groups,
and stuff all the mailings and who volunteer
at the drop of a hat –
the gift of your time and talent
is deeply appreciated.

I thank
my husband Joe
and my children Lisa, Mark, and Susan
whose loving support and willing sacrifices
made it possible for me to be Amanda the Panda.

Dedicated to

my husband Joe,
my children Lisa, Mark, and Susan,
and their spouses Dean and Denise,
who have encouraged the writing of this book,

and to

my twin sons Tommy and David,
who died at birth but will always live
in a special place in my heart.

We are at our greatest
when we inspire,
encourage,
and connect
with another human being.

Maya Angelou

Introduction

In the course of history and in one's lifetime, there are many happenings; some of them are good and we rejoice and consider ourselves blessed. Others are not so good and we struggle to make sense of them.

When a natural disaster or a personal tragedy occurs, we often wonder why or how a good God could let this happen. Certainly, the terminal illness and death of a child would fall in this category.

We usually don't consider natural disasters like a tsunami or floods and hurricanes something to rejoice about. Instead, we focus on the devastation left in their wake and the people left homeless and hungry and searching for their loved ones.

The images of 169,000 people killed by a tsunami in southeast Asia, the terrorist attack of 9/11, the war in Iraq, the Florida hurricanes, and so many other events in our history and in our lives are overwhelming and leave our hearts aching and our global spirit crushed. And, rightfully so, if our focus ended with the television images etched in our minds and hearts. But there is so much more that speaks of hope, not disaster. In every event or happening, hope is present.

Hope may come in the response of millions of people – many of them strangers, whose immediate response to a natural disaster is, "What can I do to help?" It may come in the phone call from a neighbor in the middle of the night who sees your light on and knows that you are struggling. It may come in the hand of a friend who stops by to give a hug or bring a meal.

Some might view this book as a book about children who died. It is so much more than that. To focus only on their death does not do justice to the way they lived. Often, when a loved one dies, families focus on the day they died, instead of the years they lived.

One focus is life-giving; the other is not.

This is a book about the indomitable spirit of children; it is about their faith and courage and beauty. It is about hope that makes all things bearable in the midst of pain and suffering. It is about the legacy left by some truly incredible children whose lives and death can teach us so much about living.

It is my hope that, as you read these stories, you will focus on the children's lives and the way they lived them and take courage from them for your own personal moments of pain and suffering.

Preface

As Amanda the Panda, I have had the profound privilege to meet some very young and remarkable children who, through their dying, taught me a lot about living and loving. Clearly, it was not a chance meeting; it was a *graced* encounter. I fell in love with them and they with me, and neither of us were ever the same because of that.

A few of the children I saw only once; others, many times over the course of six months, nine months, a year or two, and more. They had names like other children you meet: Sara, Chris, Brady, Charlie, Shani. All of them had one thing in common, they all had cancer in one form or another: leukemia, rhabdomyosarcoma, Wilm's tumors, brain tumors, medulloblastomas.

When I first met them, they were cancer patients who happened to be children. As I fell in love with them, they became children who happened to have cancer. Most of the children were seven and eight years old; some were a little younger, others were a bit older. They all wiggled their way deep into my heart where they continue to live today.

All of them were wise beyond their years! They had so much courage, love, hope, and faith. They were very matter-of-fact and refreshingly honest and open, as children often are. They giggled with glee. They played with gusto when they had the energy. They were masters at reading the body language of adults around them. They knew when it was okay to share their fears and when it was not, as well as whom they could talk with about living and dying and whom they could not.

They gifted me with all of the above and so much more. They shared their laughter with me and honored me with their tears. Through them, I learned a lot about life, love, courage, faith, celebrating moments, and telling people you love them before it's too late. Through them, I saw the face of God.

I have written down their stories to the best of my ability.

They are true stories. As you read them, may your heart be forever touched by their honesty, their hope, and their courage, and may their dying teach you about living.

Their stories are a gift to you from my heart, the heart of a bear.

JoAnn Zimmerman

Chapter 1
The Question

"Here I am, Lord. Is it I, Lord? I have heard you calling in the night. I will go, Lord, if you lead me. I will hold your people in my heart." St. Louis Jesuits

If you could do ANYTHING you wanted with the rest of your life, what would it be? That was the question that haunted me in the springtime of my 39th year. It surfaced from the depth of my heart and the core of my being. The question was relentless.

At first I tried to dismiss it, rationalizing that I already had a good job that I enjoyed. I was a wife and mother of three young children who more than filled my time and made my life meaningful. I was active in volunteer work in my community. God was a priority in my life, and I made time each year to get away for eight days of silence to listen to Him speak to my heart. In my 39th year, I had settled into the "routine" of my life, and it was good.

But the question would not go away. It had grabbed hold of me like a race car driver holds on to the steering wheel of his race car as he travels at record speeds and around curves that would make most of us spin out of control. I couldn't shake loose from it, and I couldn't ignore it any longer either. Could it be coming from God? It was time to give the question its due respect.

I asked for guidance and clarity as I began prayerfully reflecting on my life and who I was before God. I asked myself what I valued most; what made me uniquely me; what gifts God had blessed me with; what might He be calling me to, and why now? There was a lot to consider and pray about, and the answer would not come in a mere day or two.

Much of prayer for me has been listening to God speak to my heart where my deepest longings are - where integrity, truth, honesty, and humility reside side by side, and where there is no hiding before God.

That was the backdrop from which I wrestled with the haunting question: If you could do anything you wanted with the rest of your life, what would it be? As I began reflecting on my life and what gifts God had blessed me with in abundance, two very specific gifts surfaced over and over.

The first one was love for children. I love all children; they are very life-giving for me, from infants to toddlers and young children to teens. Each age brings so many joys and challenges. I have loved being a mother to my own children and now am thoroughly enjoying my young grandchildren. The second gift that God has blessed me with abundantly is the gift of a compassionate heart.

Music is another means of prayer for me, and a song by the St. Louis Jesuits entitled, *Here I Am, Lord,* also touched me deeply as I was reflecting on all the questions that were racing through my mind. The words that spoke to me were, "Here I am, Lord. Is it I, Lord? I have heard you calling in the night. I will go, Lord, if you lead me. I will hold your people in my heart."

Now I was closer to the answer. Whatever I was going to do with the rest of my life would clearly involve children, compassion, and heart. I wasn't certain yet of the form this would take, but I knew the matter. It was now becoming ever clearer.

I would use my gifts of compassion and love for children to be a caring presence in the community and to be present to young people who were hurting in hospitals or in their homes. I would help sensitize children to care for one another, especially if a classmate were different from them in some way. I would teach children to be compassionate, caring, and sensitive to the needs of those around them. And I would do it with the compassionate heart that God had given me.

Now the question was, "How do I go from my current paying job to being a caring presence in the community?" I wanted to do this in the form of a costumed character, much like the Disneyland characters or high school and college mascots.

Two Different Approaches

I approached the savings and loan that I worked for to see if they would like to "sponsor" the concept. We would create our own costumed character, preferably an animal, and wherever the animal went, my employer would get the credit and visibility, and I would be the animal.

I outlined what the costumed character would do and what it would not do. It would not open savings accounts or wear the name of the institution on its back like a bowling shirt. It would simply be a caring presence in the community. It would go to hospitals and nursing homes and visit people who were seriously ill in their homes.

I sent my proposal to the marketing department and received an interview soon afterwards. My interview turned out to be an exercise in frustration and miscommunication. It went very much like this:

Marketing:	That is a great idea; it is very creative! We like it! Is it entirely your idea?
Me:	Yes, it is.
Marketing:	We have given your idea much thought since we first received your proposal and we discussed it in department meetings and with management prior to today's meeting. We would like you to consider being a dollar bill with legs.
Me:	Excuse me? A dollar bill with legs?
Marketing:	Yes.
Me:	I don't think so. That is so commercial! I want to be an animal.
Marketing:	Do you feel strongly about that?
Me:	Yes, very strongly!
Marketing:	Okay, then, if you don't like the dollar bill idea and want to be an animal, would you consider being a bull?
Me:	A bull?
Marketing:	Yes, a bull would be very appropriate and symbolic of financial institutions. A bull represents stocks; stocks represent the stock market; the stock market represents financial institutions; and financial institutions represent banks and savings and loans. It would be perfect.

Me:	That wasn't exactly what I had in mind. I was thinking more like a panda bear that would be warm, cuddly, and even playful and could give bear hugs. Children often take their teddy bears to bed with them at night and cuddle with them and entrust them with their hopes and fears and even with their secrets. Their bears help them feel safe and secure.
	We could take the lovableness of a panda into the greyer areas of life where children get sick and sometimes die. I also want to go into schools and teach children how to care for one another, especially if there is a child who is different from them in one way or another.
Marketing:	(Totally ignoring the idea of a panda and the importance of bears to children) That's a great idea! We could send you into schools to teach the difference between banks and savings and loans.
Me:	Folks, this meeting is ended. We are on totally different wave lengths here. You are not hearing what I am saying, and I totally reject what I hear you saying! Whether you support me or not, you will see a bear on the streets of Des Moines.

I worked there long enough to save the money to have a panda costume made, and then I resigned my position and gave birth to Amanda the Panda, the bear with a heart.

The costume was perfect. It was a warm and friendly panda bear costume and it was beautiful. It had a very friendly face and conveyed an image that was playful, gentle, loving, and trustworthy. The costume had long black and white fur that was very warm for Iowa's harsh winters and a separate soft, red velvet heart that hung around the neck with a long, red velvet cord.

The heart would be something the children could snuggle up

to; it would be an outward sign of a loving bear. The children would know that each of them had a special place in Amanda's heart - forever.

Then, the heart was brand new, but in time it would become torn and tattered and would hang together by a single thread. That would be the price to pay for falling in love with children who would wiggle their way deep into Amanda's heart and later, die.

At that point, I was not aware of the emotional price I would pay. I was eager to put on the costume and become Amanda the Panda, the bear with a heart. November 11, 1980, was the beginning of an incredible journey that has lasted for more than two and a half decades and gifted me with the love and trust of thousands of children whose faith, spirit, courage, and trust in God have been astounding and inspiring. I have been richly blessed!

JoAnn and Amanda in 1980

Chapter 2
Chris

"You're my pal, Amanda, forever and for always." Chris, age seven

Amanda's first friend was Chris. He was referred to her from Hospice of Central Iowa. He was seven years old and had an inoperable brain tumor. Chris had a bulging eye with a cloudy film over it. When he walked, his leg dragged and his arm was paralyzed. He was so thin that he wore red suspenders to hold his jeans up. In his face you could see his gentle nature.

Amanda fell in love with him, hook, line, and sinker. And he fell deeply in love with Amanda. Chris would live only five more months from the day Amanda first met him. In those few months, Amanda visited him at home and in the hospital more than forty times.

Amanda's first visit to Chris took place in his home. It was a bitter cold January day. The snow had recently been shoveled from the sidewalk leading to his front door. There was a large picture window in the front room with the curtains wide open to let the sunshine in. On days that Chris was feeling a little better, he could lie on the couch, look out the window, and watch the snow fall or other children on their way to school. If Chris was watching, his classmates would wave to him as they walked by. On this cold day, Chris was watching from the couch as Amanda sauntered up to his front door and rang his doorbell.

He had just been released from the hospital earlier that afternoon and still had his red pajamas and blue bathrobe on as he sat on the couch by the window. It felt so good to be home again!

His small, tidy, living room was filled to capacity during that first visit. His mother, stepfather, brother, sister, grandparents, the hospice volunteer, and his beloved great-grandmother were all there to welcome him home. There were more people than chairs in the living room on that day. Chris's mother brought in chairs from the kitchen so all the adults could sit down while his brother and sister played on the floor nearby. Every available inch of space in that tiny living room seemed occupied by the people who loved Chris so much.

On the kitchen table was a large plate filled with Chris's favorite cookies and hot chocolate with marshmallows for anyone who was still chilled from the bitter cold outside. You could feel the love in the room and the joy everyone felt that he was finally home again!

Chris sitting on Amanda's lap

Chris was very excited to meet Amanda. Their first visit was brief because all the excitement of his welcome home party and seeing all his relatives and friends had left Chris very tired and needing to rest.

Amanda and Chris barely got to know one another that day. As she left his home, Amanda left her card with him and told him that if he ever needed her - day or night - to just call and she would be there. As she left, she asked Chris if he would draw her a picture when he felt better. "Yes, Amanda. I love to draw!" he said, with a tiny voice that reflected how tiring his trip home from the hospital had been for him.

A few weeks later, his mother phoned Amanda and told her that Chris would like to see her and that he had drawn a picture and was excited to share it with her. Amanda could hardly wait to see Chris again and to see his drawing. She left immediately for the short ride across town to Chris's house.

Symbolic Drawing

When she arrived at his home, he was looking out the window watching for her. His mother opened the door and he came right over to her as if they were life-long friends, climbed up on her lap, and proudly showed her his two-page, black and white drawing. This time, his voice was strong and he was dressed in street clothes instead of his red pajamas. He had on a white shirt, jeans, and red suspenders attached to his jeans.

Amanda noticed that the first page of his drawing showed a long semi-truck with one of its wheels loose and a tiny little boy in the cab of the truck. The truck almost resembled a hospital bed. On the second page, Chris had drawn a large house, and in the upper left hand corner of the paper he had written the words, "Amanda the Panda's House."

Chris snuggled into Amanda's lap and she asked him to tell her all about his drawing.

"This is a truck, Amanda, and I am driving the truck," he said, "but there's something wrong with the wheel of my truck. The wheel on the right is loose and because it's loose, it won't take me where I want to go; so I get out of my truck and I fix the wheel and

9

then I drive all the way over to Amanda the Panda's house. But when I get there, she's not home. And when she finds out that I drove all the way over to her house and she wasn't home, she drives all the way over to my house, but I'm not home!"

"Why do we keep missing each other, Chris?" Amanda asked him, puzzled. "Why am I not home when you come to my house and you're not home when I come to yours?"

Chris did not have an answer to her question; he simply didn't know why. Amanda wondered if it was because they had not had a chance yet during their first visit to talk about things that Chris wanted to talk about. They were *missing each other*! From his drawing, Amanda understood that she was going to be an important "person" in his life.

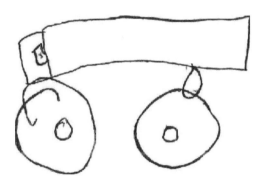

Page one of Chris's drawing: The Truck

Page two: Amanda the Panda's house

10

Becoming A Member Of The Family

Over the course of the next forty visits to his home and hospital room, Amanda became a full-fledged member of his entire family, from his delightful great-grandmother who asked Amanda to call her "Grandma" to his younger brother and sister.

His beloved great-grandmother also had cancer and needed surgery, but kept postponing it because she felt that dealing with Chris's illness was more crucial than taking care of her own medical needs. She thought she would have plenty of time after Chris died to schedule her own surgery. However, that was not the case. Her doctor informed her that they could wait no longer, and Grandma underwent surgery in the same hospital where Chris was a patient. She was in intensive care downstairs and Chris was upstairs on the fourth floor of the same hospital.

Bear Visits Intensive Care

One evening, after being with Chris for a few hours, Amanda decided to visit Grandma in intensive care. It was well past visiting hours, nearly 10:00 P.M. Not knowing where intensive care was, Amanda wandered down to the first floor and asked someone at the information desk if she could visit intensive care at this hour and where it might be. The woman at the desk replied, "Lady, looking like that you could go *anywhere* in this hospital." She proceeded to give Amanda instructions to the elevators and the lower level where she would find intensive care.

Amanda thanked the woman and proceeded to intensive care to find Grandma. They had a wonderful visit, and, as Amanda was preparing to leave, two nurses approached her and asked if she would mind visiting one more patient, a man named Herman.

Herman had been in intensive care for several days and was feeling rather blue. They thought that a visit from Amanda would cheer him up. Amanda was happy to oblige.

The nurses took her to see Herman, a man in his late seventies who was obviously very ill. He was hooked up to IV's and monitors, and his room was not far from the nurse's station. They seemed to come in frequently to check on him. Herman's wife kept a constant vigil by his side from 8:00 in the morning until 9:00 at

11

night. Then she would go home to sleep in her own bed and return each morning to be with her husband of fifty-five years. She was not in the best of health, and the long days took a toll on her, too. Herman was as concerned about her as she was about him.

Amanda sat on the edge of his bed and held his hand. Herman seemed to enjoy Amanda's visit, and they chatted briefly about a variety of things. He told Amanda that he wished his wife were there to meet Amanda, too. He knew that she would like Amanda instantly. Amanda gave Herman a very gentle hug and assured him that she would return to see him the next evening when she came back to see Grandma. They said goodbye, Amanda went home, and Herman fell asleep.

He awoke in the middle of the night on the *next* shift. Right away, he began telling the nurses, "There was a bear in my room last night." (No one from the previous shift had documented his chart that he had had a furry visitor the night before, so the nurses on this shift knew nothing about it.) They listened to him and tried repeatedly to assure Herman that there was no bear in his room last night. Herman became increasingly agitated because they wouldn't believe him. Frustrated, he decided to wait until morning when his wife was present to say any more about the friendly bear who came to visit him in the night.

The next morning, a new and third shift of nurses was at his bedside when his wife arrived. Again, he began talking about the bear in his room. He told his wife and the nurses, "There was a bear in my room last night. It was a nice bear, sat on the edge of my bed right where you are sitting and held my hand." No one believed him! He continued, "It was a big bear, black and white and it had a big red heart around its neck! It was a friendly bear! I think it was a female bear."

The nurses and his wife looked at one another and shook their heads, convinced that Herman was hallucinating. The nurses called his doctor and had his medications changed so that his hallucinations would stop!

The next evening, when Amanda arrived in intensive care to visit Grandma, she asked the nurses how Herman was. They explained, "For seventeen hours, he has been trying to convince his wife and the nurses that you were here! Would you visit him again, please?"

After seeing him again and assuring him that he was not hallucinating, Amanda told Herman all about a special little boy on the fourth floor that she had fallen in love with whose name was Chris.

A Special Connection

Chris was incredibly bright and terribly polite. He always made formal introductions, introducing his "very best friend, Amanda" to anyone who would come into his hospital room. "You're my pal, Amanda, forever and for always," he would say to her. And she would reply, "That's right, Chris, forever and for always you will live in my heart."

In those visits, simple and profound conversations took place. The boy and the bear connected on such a deep level of trust where anything said was listened to and given its proper importance and value. The two of them became nearly inseparable. They always hugged ever so gently so as not to hurt his very frail, thin body. Each visit ended with panda bear kisses – a little boy and a giant panda bear rubbing noses.

Chris knew that Amanda also visited other children with cancer. He would always ask her three questions about the other children. He wanted to know what kind of cancer they had; if they had lost their hair, too; and what their prognosis was.

People Who Are Unconscious Can Hear

One day after visiting children in another town and on her way back to Des Moines, Amanda stopped by the hospital to visit Chris. As she walked into his room, his mother told her that Chris was in a coma. She was sitting by his bedside looking very tired and weary. Her love and concern for her son were very apparent. She looked as if she could collapse at any moment. Amanda asked her if she would like a break and told her that she would stay with Chris for a few hours so she could go home to take a nap or a shower or just have a change of pace.

As his mother left, Amanda sat down by his bedside, held his hand, and began to tell Chris about the other children she had seen that day. She answered all the questions Chris would have asked if he were not in a coma. She got no response from Chris, but deep down she knew he could hear her.

Later, a nurse stopped by his room to visit with him for a while. Again, there was no conscious response from Chris. As the nurse was leaving, she said to him, "I've got to go now, Chris. I have other patients to see, but I'll be back. See ya later, alligator."

In a very small, sweet voice, barely audible, Chris replied, "After a while, crocodile."

During those forty visits, a friend became concerned about Amanda and the deep relationship that was developing between her and Chris. Out of love, he said to her, "You are getting too close to Chris. What are you going to do when he dies?"

She replied, "I don't know, but I call myself the 'bear with a heart,' and my heart has to be a heart of flesh, not of stone. Hearts of flesh fall in love, hurt, cry, bleed, and sometimes die a little themselves. I couldn't do this any other way. It's heartbreaking at times, but love is always worth the dying."

Symbolic Language

Children don't have a language to deal with death and dying the way adults do. Oftentimes, they use art to convey what is going on inside them, and when they speak, they use *symbolic* language.

Chris and Amanda had many conversations about his future, and one day Chris spoke to Amanda of his final trip, using symbolic language.

He said, "I am going on a trip, Amanda, and I want you to go with me."

"Where are we going, Chris?" Amanda asked.

"We are going to go on an airplane ride. We are going to go way high above the clouds. And the clouds are going to be very soft and pillowy, and it is going to be really neat!"

From this conversation and more like it, Amanda knew that Chris was not afraid to die and he was beginning to say goodbye.

An Unforgettable Birthday Celebration

For months before his eighth birthday, Chris had been talking about the birthday party he wanted and how his hospital room would be decorated with balloons and streamers. He wanted a special cake, big enough to serve all his friends. He began making his guest list. Everyone was invited because everyone who knew Chris was his friend - all the nurses, doctors, lab techs, his school bus driver, his family, and Amanda.

With all the preparations duly recorded on paper as per his wishes, he could relax. He knew that everything would be taken care of. In fact, on the day of his birthday, April 22, he was not able to blow out his candles or eat his cake or pop the balloons. Chris was unconscious again; he had been for four days. But that did not stop his mother from fulfilling his wish to have a party just as he had prescribed. All of his friends gathered in his hospital room to honor and celebrate with a very special little boy on his eighth birthday. His room was filled with balloons and streamers, and the cake was large enough to serve everyone.

A Profound, Spiritual Moment

After the party, his friends began to say their goodbyes and to leave, one by one. The only people left in his room were his closest friends: his mother, his school bus driver, the driver's wife, and Amanda. It was past 10:00 P.M. when the nurses came into his room to change his bed. One of the nurses asked if anyone wanted to hold him while they changed the sheets.

Amanda wanted to in the worst way, but didn't feel it would be appropriate for her since his mother was there and the honor rightfully belonged to her. She must have read Amanda's heart, because she turned to Amanda and said, "Amanda, *you* hold him."

Amanda, who had been standing at Chris's bedside, sat down in a rocking chair as the nurses gently put his very frail, tiny body in her arms. She very gently and lovingly cradled his head with its bulging eye in her arms and sat there with tears streaming down her (JoAnn's) face as she said, "Chris, it is your birthday and I get the present. I get to hold you." It was a very sacred moment for Amanda. It reminded her of what it must have been like when they took Jesus' body down from the cross.

Chris died eleven days after his eighth birthday. His grandmother told Amanda that just before he died, the eye that had been cloudy became "crystal clear." She said he took three very deep breaths, smiled the most beautiful, wide smile, and then died. She thought that perhaps he was seeing his father who died just before he was born.

Perhaps he was riding on his soft and pillowy clouds and it was, as he described earlier, "really neat."

Chapter 3
Sara

"Dear God, I don't care when you decide it's time for me to go to Heaven. I know it will be a good time!" Sara, age seven

"It's hard being someone like me," wrote Sara to Amanda the Panda. "Would you come and visit me?" she asked. "I am seven years old and I have leukemia. I live in Mason City." Sara had seen a newspaper article about Amanda the Panda with Chris and knew that Amanda was a special friend to children living with cancer.

Amanda wrote back immediately, asking directions to Sara's house, telling her that she loved her letter and the red stationery on which it was written. She said that she could hardly wait to meet her and give her a great big bear hug. So began a very special love affair between a little girl with leukemia and a giant panda bear who wears a big, red velvet heart around her neck.

Although Sara and Amanda lived 120 miles apart, visits to Mason City were many throughout the next nine months. Amanda and Sara instantly became best friends.

During Amanda's first visit, Sara opened the door wide and then timidly hid behind her father's back as the giant panda entered her home. Sara wore a pretty pink dress, a scarf covering her bald head, and painted fingernails. Amanda brought gifts for Sara and her brother and sisters. It didn't take long for Sara to get comfortable with Amanda. She took her by the hand and led her to the living room where the piano was. On the piano were photos of Sara and her siblings. Sara's photo showed a pretty little girl with long, blond hair. It was taken before she became ill and lost her hair.

Sara sat down to play and asked Amanda to sit down beside her. She removed her scarf, revealing very little hair, and began to play for Amanda. She was as beautiful without hair as she was in the photo. The two of them bonded in that moment, and she never wore the scarf again in Amanda's presence.

Fun Times Together

The two of them thoroughly enjoyed each other's company. Sara would play the piano for Amanda and show her all of her toys and stuffed animals. Other times, Amanda would notice that Sara had on new fingernail polish. Sometimes they would go out to the backyard and swing on her swing set, or Sara would just sit on Amanda's lap and they would read stories together. Other times they would share special secrets that could only be entrusted to the two of them. Many times those secrets had to do with Sara's illness. There was nothing they couldn't share with each other. Sometimes they talked about dying and what Heaven might be like. Other times they discussed questions that simply had no answers. And always, they hugged!

Sara and Amanda hugging

Sara in her backyard swinging with Amanda

Child First, Cancer Patient Second

Sara was a very normal child who happened to have leukemia. Unfortunately, when children get cancer, the focus seems to be more on their cancer and less on their childhood. Their lives become a series of hospitalizations, bone marrow punctures, spinal taps, drugs, and treatments. They grow up so fast. They cross over quickly from the realm of childhood into the realm of adulthood, and their days of fun, laughter, play, silliness, giggles, and all that is childhood seem to vanish much too quickly.

Yet, inside that little body with cancer beats the heart of a child. Children need playmates, fun, laughter, and friends, especially friends who stick by them in spite of their cancer.

The Perfect Birthday Gift

One summer day in June, Sara called Amanda and invited her to come to her birthday party. She was going to be eight years old.

"What can I bring you?" asked Amanda. Sara had given a lot of thought to her birthday party and she knew exactly what she wanted! She gave Amanda her three wishes. "I'd like to have a new swing set," she said. "Or a giant panda as big as you are!" she added. "But what I *really* want is a puppy, only my mom says I can't have a dog."

Amanda assured Sara that she would be delighted to come to her birthday party, and then gave serious consideration to an appropriate gift for her special friend. Of all the possibilities she came up with, only one would bring Sara the ultimate joy - the puppy!

The next day, when Sara wasn't quite so near the telephone, Amanda called Sara's mother to discuss the puppy and how she felt about such a gift. Was it totally out of the question? Sara's mom pondered the question and all it would mean to have a puppy in the house. After some time she said, "Well, Sara has wanted a puppy for a long time, and her brother and sisters want a puppy, too. I guess Amanda could bring her a dog, but please let it be a *small* dog!"

Amanda was now almost as excited as she knew Sara would be. Immediately, she began looking for just the right dog, finally settling on a little female puppy that seemed to be part Cocker Spaniel and part *panda*. She was black and white, black and white, and black and white. Best of all, she was a *small* dog!

Amanda took the dog to a veterinarian for a check-up to make sure she was healthy, gave her a bath, and then placed her in a beautifully gift-wrapped box for the two-hour drive to Mason City. The box had a big, red bow on the outside and a clean, happy, love-filled, tail-wagging puppy on the inside. It was the *perfect* gift for Sara.

When Sara saw Amanda carrying the large box with the big red bow in her arms, she could hardly contain her excitement. She had no idea what was inside. She ran out the front door to meet her, gave her a great big hug, and immediately wanted to open the box. She threw open the lid to the box and her face was filled with surprise and excitement. She never dreamed it would be a puppy. She was absolutely thrilled and immediately named the dog, who quickly became her constant companion, "Pandy."

Sara's birthday party was everything a child's birthday party should be: friends, fun, presents, laughter, excitement, cake, ice cream, and games. For the moment, Sara was a normal eight-year-old girl surrounded by lots of friends celebrating her birthday with a brand new puppy by her side.

Except for a few tell-tale signs such as the loss of hair and the effects of the steroid prednisone, which made her face puffy, no one would have suspected that this child had cancer.

Celebrating Moments

When children have cancer, families and friends learn to celebrate the moments. They don't look too far ahead. Tomorrow is too uncertain, and there is no guarantee that tomorrow will even come. *TODAY* is what is important. That is why every effort was made to make her birthday party so special.

Later that month, just a few short weeks after her eighth birthday, Sara's body suffered another major setback; the drugs and treatments she was receiving were no longer able to control her leukemia which caused her to relapse again. In July she had to undergo a series of painful spinal taps.

She wrote to Amanda again and asked her to be present during those dreaded weekly spinal taps. "Ow-ie, ow-ie, ow-ie," she cried, as Amanda held her hand. "Ow-ie, ow-ie, ow-ie!" Each time Sara cried out, Amanda's heart would break a little inside.

Those Wednesdays were almost as hard on Amanda as they were on Sara. Certainly, they were the worst Wednesdays of Amanda's life. Yet, her mother said, "Sara almost looks forward to them, because she knows that Amanda will be right there with her." The spinal taps took place every Wednesday for three consecutive weeks.

On Wednesday of the second week, as Amanda was going into the hospital to be with Sara, she noticed an elderly gentleman sitting on a chair outside the entrance to the hospital. He was talking to some people who were standing beside him. She thought nothing of it. He wasn't there when she left to go back to Des Moines. But on the third Wednesday, there he was again. This time he flagged Amanda down.

"I have seen you coming here for the past three weeks," he told her, "and I have been sitting here hoping to catch you each time because I want to ask you if you do children's birthday parties?"

"No," said Amanda, "unless your child is ill. You see, you have many other options available to you. Children with cancer do not." The man understood what Amanda was saying and she never saw him again.

The hardest part of being Sara's friend was to watch her suffer and not be able to do anything to take her pain away or to lessen it. It was so hard for these two special friends to be together in all that suffering, but to not be there was out of the question; it was unthinkable. After all, they both knew that a friend is one who stands by you in good times and in bad.

During her spinal taps, Sara tried to focus on Amanda instead of her pain. She would look very intently at Amanda, as the bear with a heart sat close beside her and held her hand. One day Sara actually discovered *Amanda's (JoAnn's)* eyes. She was so excited and exclaimed, "Amanda! I see *YOUR* eyes! Are you *CRYING* or are you *sweating?*" Amanda (JoAnn) was doing both.

After the spinal taps were over, Sara had to lie still for a period of time so that she didn't get severe headaches by getting up too quickly. During those times, she and Amanda would play word search games to pass the time away.

Sara and her incredible smile
(Photo taken after a painful spinal tap)

Her Final Relapse

By the end of July, after all the spinal taps were completed, the doctor called a meeting with Sara's parents to discuss what further treatments might be prescribed. The news was not good. He offered them very little hope, giving them only two options. The first was to discontinue all treatments. The second was to try an experimental drug that had been tried before with other children with the same type of leukemia as Sara's, with only a flicker of a positive response.

Sara was in a corner of the room, crying softly as her parents discussed their options with the doctor. He heard her soft cries and looked over at her with great sensitivity and tenderness. He asked her to tell him what she was thinking, because, after all, it was her life and her future they were discussing. Sara looked at her doctor, then at her parents, and back at the doctor. She shook her little head as she responded, "They don't want to know what I'm thinking. I don't want any more spinal taps or any more drugs or treatments. I want to be in Heaven with Jesus and Heather and Grandpa Van and Ritchie. I want to die."

Good News/Bad News

Sara understood well what relapses meant. Early in her leukemia she would ask hard questions, and her parents always answered them honestly.

"Daddy, if I have relapse after relapse, will I die?" she asked her dad one day.

"Yes," he answered her.

"But I don't want to die," she replied.

"Honey, we don't want you to die, either," he responded, holding her close to his heart, his eyes filling with tears.

Sara was quiet for a few moments as she thought about what her father had said. Then she replied, "But I have good news and bad news. The good news is that when I die I will go to Heaven and see Grandpa Van and Ritchie (her two-month-old brother who died of heart disease) and Jesus. But the bad news is that I have to die first."

Sara had also written prayers to God about dying. Many of

them were written after relapses. Once she wrote, "Dear God, I don't care when you decide when it will be time for me to go to Heaven. I know it will be a good time!"

Sara had given a lot of thought to dying. She also prayed a lot about it. She was not afraid to die. She really wanted to be reunited with her best friend Heather, who had died a few months earlier. When Heather died, Amanda called Sara's mother and asked her how Sara was doing with her friend's death. Sara's mother said Sara had a creative writing book at home which asked various questions, and Sara would complete the answers by filling in the blanks. One question was, "If I had one wish, it would be _____," and Sara wrote, "to die."

Sara's Drawing Of Heaven

She and Heather, who also had cancer and was a special friend of Amanda's, had met at the hospital during their treatments. After Heather died and about six weeks before her own death, Sara drew a picture of Heaven and Earth separated by a line across the middle of the page. Below the line was Earth with Sara's mom and dad and her house. Her mom was saying, "We love you, Sara," and her dad was saying, "Amen!!"

Sara was so deeply loved that she even accentuated that fact in her drawing by putting two exclamation points after her father's "Amen." Above the line was Heaven.

Sara's concept of Heaven was that she was going to sit on a throne and be crowned. She drew herself sitting on a chair with a tiny little yellow crown above her head and the word *me* by her feet. Sara wanted to make sure that everyone understood that this was to be *her* crown. In Heaven with her were three people; one of them was her best friend Heather.

Sara's drawing of Heaven

Honesty And Openness – The Greatest Gifts

Sara's parents were always honest and open with her about her leukemia. She knew everything there was to know about the disease. She knew about remissions and relapses, and she understood the possibility that she might die if her body kept relapsing.

Her parents created a very open environment where it was okay for Sara to talk about *any* concerns or fears she might have about anything, including dying. This openness to honestly and lovingly discuss any topic with her helped to dispel all fears she might have had. Sara was not afraid to die.

One day Sara's father, an attorney, explained to Sara that when people get ready to die, they often like to make out a will so that they can leave certain possessions to specific people. He asked her if she would like to make out a will. Sara thought seriously about all her worldly possessions. Then she replied, "No, I would rather have people choose what they want - that way they're sure to get the right thing. But I *do* have a last wish. I'd like to have my fingernails painted so I will look pretty in the casket."

If her parents had not created an environment in which she could talk openly about her dying, they never would have known that she had a very specific last wish. When Sara died, Amanda was privileged to help make her last wish come true. She brought the fingernail polish so she would "look pretty in the casket."

Honoring Sara's Decision

Sara was firm in her decision to have no more drugs or treatments. She really wanted them stopped. Reluctantly and with a heavy heart, her parents took her wishes into consideration, discontinued all treatments, and brought Sara home. Sara was very happy. "The happiest she had ever been," her mother said. The next few weeks went by too quickly.

Her parents took Sara on a short vacation to the lakes in northern Minnesota where her grandparents had a cabin. They took her boating and fishing. She soaked up the sun and played in the sand. She was surrounded by her family, grandparents, uncles, aunts, and cousins. They packed as much living in those few weeks as possible and took full advantage of the days that Sara felt well. But the time was far too short. Sara started to get sick and weak, and it was time to take her home.

The Final Phone Call

On a Sunday evening, around midnight, the telephone rang at Amanda's house. It was Sara's dad.

"Amanda, we just want you to know that Sara is not doing very well now," he said. "She can't keep any food down, is losing weight, and is now confined to her room. She even needs a wheelchair to get to the bathroom. We have been trying to reach you for a few days. We knew you would want to know."

Amanda explained that she had just returned early from a short vacation out of state. They talked more about Sara, but Amanda didn't fully comprehend how close Sara was to dying. Perhaps, in her heart, she just wasn't ready yet to let her go.

After hanging up the telephone, Amanda got very little sleep that night as she went over and over in her mind every detail of her conversation with Sara's father. A haunting question kept tugging at her heart, "Why would Sara's dad call at midnight if it weren't more serious than her heart was willing to acknowledge?"

Early the next morning, Amanda called Sara's home seeking more information and dreading what she might learn. Sara's mother answered the telephone. "Jayne, how is Sara? What is really happening?" she asked. Jayne told her that last Wednesday the doctors had given Sara one week more to live. It was now Monday of the following week! Amanda asked Jayne if she and Sara would like her to come right away.

Unusual Request

When Jayne asked Sara if she wanted Amanda to come, Sara had a most unusual reply. "YES!" she said, "And tell her to bring her *family!*"

Amanda was confused by Sara's response. What could Sara mean? Never once in their nine-month love affair had Sara asked about or even mentioned Amanda's (JoAnn's) own family. It seemed strange that Sara would say, "YES! And tell her to bring her *family!*" That would be like a child meeting Santa Claus and asking him to come and bring his family!

Perplexed, she decided to take JoAnn and JoAnn's oldest daughter Lisa with her to Mason City. They picked up the panda costume from the dry cleaners and headed directly to Mason City. Within two hours, Amanda walked into Sara's bedroom.

Sara's Reaction

When Sara saw Amanda, she immediately began to cry. She had not been crying before Amanda entered her room. Amanda was surprised by this and didn't understand the cause for her tears, so she asked Sara why she was crying.

Between sobs, Sarah replied, "Oh, I wanted you to bring *YOU* this time! I wanted to see *YOU*!"

Suddenly, it all made sense. Sara was the most inquisitive child Amanda had ever known. She constantly wondered about Amanda's true identity and who was in the costume. Amanda recalled Sara's delight the moment she saw Amanda's (JoAnn's) eyes during one of those awful spinal taps and asked if she were crying or sweating. Amanda sensed that Sara knew this would be her last opportunity to see the person behind the bear and that's why she was sobbing.

"Sweetheart, don't cry," Amanda said. "We can fix that. In fact, that's easy to fix. Promise me you won't laugh, count to three, and I'll remove my head."

Sara immediately stopped crying and counted to three. Amanda kept her promise and removed her panda head. There was total silence in the room as Sara looked at her faithful friend of nine months, only to see JoAnn's face. The silence seemed to last forever.

Finally, Sara spoke. "OH!" she said, as she gazed at *JoAnn's* face on Amanda's body. After a very long pause, Sara added, "Amanda, would you put your head back on, please?"

Amanda put her head back on. After a short while, Sara said, "No, Amanda, take your head off and be with me awhile." Amanda took her head off and put it on the chair beside Sara's bed.

A Long Night

Throughout the night, these two friends stayed together, silently loving each other, just being in each other's presence. Amanda/JoAnn listened to Sara's final prayer, "Dear God, I know that you love us and I love you. You know I love you a lot because you are my father, my dear father. Dear Lord, take this leukemia away from me. It bothers me."

Amanda/JoAnn stayed with Sara until three o'clock in the morning. Then, when Sara was sleeping, JoAnn went into the next room to lie down, leaving her panda head close beside Sara the entire night. Towards morning, Sara became very ill and was vomiting. JoAnn walked quietly into her room and stood beside her. Sara looked at JoAnn and said, "You know what? Amanda stayed *all night* with me!"

Permission To Die

Early the next morning, Sara died. She died a beautiful death surrounded by her family and her beloved dog, Pandy.

Sarah's parents had been praying for three days that God would give them a sign that this would be her last day. At three o'clock early Wednesday morning, Sara sat up in bed in a lot of pain and said, "I hear voices!"

"What do you hear, Sara, what do you hear?" they asked.

"They are calling me to play," she answered. That was the first sign. The second sign was that she sneezed, and in the process of sneezing, she had a nosebleed that wouldn't stop. The third and final sign was that when she closed her eyes, they began to roll back. Her parents knew that this would be Sara's last day.

They asked her if she wanted to have company later in the morning and she said no.

Then she asked, "Daddy, when will I die?"

"Soon, sweetheart," he said, "very soon."

"Just try to relax your body and it won't be long now," her mother added.

Then, as hard as it was, Sara's dad gave her permission to die. "Sara, we love you so VERY, VERY MUCH and we are going to miss you more than you will ever know! But we want you to know, Sara, that it's *okay* to die. It is *OKAY* to die."

Later, one by one, Sara's brother and two sisters came in to say goodbye to Sara. Grandma and Pandy were there, too.

Towards morning, Sara said, "I've got to go now, Daddy."

"It's okay, sweetheart, go ahead and go," he replied, "We love you so much!" And she died. It was exactly two weeks to the day from when she insisted on having no more treatments.

The Funeral

When a child dies, the funeral is usually packed. Often, it is standing room only, and the church is filled with relatives, friends, and classmates.

JoAnn attended Sara's funeral and the luncheon that followed in the church basement. It was a very hot day in August, and JoAnn was wearing a short-sleeved dress. Not only would it have been inappropriate for Amanda to be at the funeral because her presence would have been a great distraction to many, but also it would have been *beastly* hot in a panda bear costume!

There were so many people at Sara's funeral that the line for the luncheon in the church basement following the funeral was a very long, slow moving line. As they waited in line, people began to chat with one another, often introducing themselves to the people in front or in back of them.

A woman with a young child in front of JoAnn turned and extended her hand to JoAnn saying, "Hi, my name is Barbara and this is my son Timothy. We are friends of Sara's parents, and Timmy went to school with Sara."

JoAnn responded by introducing herself and simply stating that she was a friend of Sara's.

The woman asked if JoAnn lived in Mason City or attended this church.

"No," she stated simply, "I am from Des Moines."

"Well, how did you know Sara if you are from Des Moines?" she asked. She was a very inquisitive woman!

In a very quiet, soft voice, JoAnn said, "I am Amanda the Panda."

In a very *loud* voice, the woman replied, "*YOU* are AMANDA

THE PANDA?" (Anyone who knew Sara knew how special Amanda was to her.)

At that point, her little boy came over to JoAnn and began gently and repeatedly stroking her arm. "*What* is he doing?" JoAnn asked Barbara.

"He heard you were Amanda the Panda and he wants to feel your fur!" she replied.

The Cemetery

Months before Sara died, her parents went to the cemetery to pick out a final resting place to bury their daughter; they looked around at several different plots. Not knowing why, Sara's mother was irresistibly drawn to one particular spot. Sara's dad suggested they look around some more. They did, but Sara's mom kept coming back to the same spot. "This is where I want Sara buried," she said.

Sara's dad agreed and together they made all the arrangements and filled out the necessary papers. Days later when they got the cemetery papers back, they discovered that the place where Sara is buried is called *CROWN HILL*!

Sara's mother recalled Sara's drawing just weeks before her death in which she had drawn herself in Heaven with a little yellow crown on her head and the words *me* by her feet. As Sara's mother put the cemetery papers away, she pondered all these things in her heart.

Sara with her new puppy, "Pandy"

Chapter 4
Some Children Know
When They Are Going To Die

Children with cancer grow up way too soon. They are wise beyond their years, and there is something about them that sets them apart from their peers. The late Elisabeth Kubler-Ross, psychiatrist and author acclaimed worldwide for her work with dying patients, said that we are all made up of four quadrants: physical, spiritual, emotional, and intellectual and, for most of us, the spiritual quadrant is the last to fully develop and mature. However, for children facing life-threatening illnesses, the very opposite is true; the spiritual quadrant is the first to develop.

Amanda witnessed this in all the children she was privileged to know. All of them were mature way beyond their peers. There was just such a special quality about them. And, not only did some children know *that* they were going to die, some children also knew *when* they were going to die.

Heather
"For the first few days when I get to Heaven, I am just going to play. Then I am going to look up and hold all the babies in Heaven." Heather, age seven

One of Sara's closest friends was Heather, a beautiful, seven-year-old girl with cancer. They would see each other on clinic days and in the hospital, and though they lived about thirty miles apart, their families would visit one another frequently. These two little girls became the best of friends.

The faith of these children was remarkable and truly inspiring. It was Good Friday and Heather was suffering a great deal and in a lot of pain. She could find no position to sit or lie in that would give her any comfort. She began to cry.

As her father held her and tried to comfort her, he thought of the "cross" she was carrying. Then he told her that Someone else suffered a great deal on this same day, many, many years ago. His name was Jesus.

Heather looked up at her father and simply said, "I know. And that means that I ought to have a good day on Sunday!" And she did! On Easter Sunday she was pain free. She died on Easter Monday.

Before she died, Heather told her mother and father that she would be going to Heaven soon and for them to not be sad because she would be happy with Jesus and she would be praying for them. She said that when she got to Heaven, for the first two days she was just going to play. (She had not been able to play for a very long time.) After that, she was going to look up and hold all the babies in Heaven. Then she said, "And you know what, Dad? When I fall off my bike in Heaven, it won't even hurt!"

Charlie

"I won't be here when you come back, Amanda." Charlie, age nine

Another child who knew *when* he was going to die was Charlie, a nine-year-old boy with medulloblastoma. Charlie wanted to be a semi-truck driver when he grew up. He had a huge collection of semi-trucks and knew everything about every one of them. One of his greatest joys was a visit that Amanda had arranged for him to tour a truck dealership owned by a friend of hers.

He got to ride in the cab of a semi-truck and wear a trucker's cap as they rode around the parking lot of the truck dealership. He even got to honk the horn. He was so happy and excited as he waved to his mother and Amanda from the cab of the truck. He was riding tall. It was a dream come true for him!

Amanda visited Charlie weekly over the course of several months. Often, Charlie would bring out his entire collection of semis and they would play together. One time, Charlie wanted to paint a portrait of Amanda. She was instructed to "sit very still so I can draw all of you." Amanda obliged.

One of their favorite things to do was to have Charlie's mother put on some of his favorite music so he and Amanda could dance around the room together. Other times they just hung out together.

One day, as they were dancing in the living room, Amanda

began to tell him that she would be leaving for a while, perhaps for three weeks to a month. (JoAnn had been in a car accident and was going to Mayo Clinic in Rochester for an evaluation and didn't know whether or not she would need surgery.) But as soon as she returned, Amanda told Charlie, he would be the first person she would visit.

Then she prepared to leave and had her paw on the door when Charlie said, "I won't be here when you come back."

Stunned, Amanda turned around and asked him, "Where will you be, Charlie?"

Charlie pointed straight up toward the sky and said, "Up there."

Charlie was saying goodbye to his good friend because he knew he would not live another three weeks. With a very heavy heart, Amanda left his home to go to Rochester with JoAnn. After many tests, it was determined that surgery was not an option for JoAnn, so Amanda returned to visit Charlie sooner than she had predicted, only to find a little boy whose body had deteriorated rapidly. Indeed, within three weeks, Charlie died.

Charlie drawing a portrait of Amanda

Mindy

"Behind every dark cloud there is a rainbow." Mindy, age nine

Another of Sara's friends was Mindy, a beautiful nine-year-old girl who waged an uphill battle against cancer for two years. Mindy had medulloblastoma, a brain tumor. Mindy's mother said her daughter's reaction to Amanda was amazing.

"It seems that there is so little Mindy gets excited about anymore – except for Amanda. She keeps her emotions under control because she has so much to cope with," her mother said.

"Mindy has had to grow up so fast because she's facing things that would give problems to most adults. But somewhere in the process of being with Amanda, she has become a child again. I've never seen her so thrilled – even with family members – as she is when she gets a call or a visit from Amanda.

"When kids learn to look forward to something more than a blood test or spinal tap, it's just beautiful, and Amanda provides that for Mindy. Amanda does more for her than a dose of medicine ever could. Amanda comes in with open arms and an 'I love you' attitude, and not just for anyone, but especially for this child.

"Amanda doesn't treat Mindy as different; she treats her as special. Mindy knows that nobody else in town has a big panda coming to visit them.

"Sometimes friends disappear fast for a child in this situation, and Amanda is special because she is faithful and loving."

Visit To Mindy's School

One day, Amanda accompanied Mindy to school. Mindy was in the third grade and had lost most of her hair. Amanda spoke to her class about friendship and what it means to be a friend – that friends don't make fun of people or call them names or laugh at them. She told the class that the *outside* of a person was just their shell and that what was inside of them was far more important than the outside. The children understood the lesson Amanda was sharing with them. All school visits ended formally with a bear hug from Amanda.

Although most of the children loved getting hugs, apparently some third grade boys are just *beginning* to find it difficult to admit publicly that they like hugs. During Mindy's school visit, Amanda asked the children if they would like a bear hug. If so, they could line up to receive one.

One little boy in the class was the first to respond. Very emphatically, he said, "No! We are too *old* for bear hugs!"

Amanda assured him that it was perfectly okay if he didn't want a bear hug, but that if anyone else in the class wanted a hug, they could line up to her left. The entire class, minus one little boy, lined up for their bear hug.

The little boy had a beautiful comeback. "Oh, what the heck," he said as he took his place at the end of the long line, "If you can't fight 'em, join 'em!"

A Breakthrough Moment

In Mindy's school, there was another class of children who were facing other challenges. Many of them were in wheelchairs, and some of them had severe emotional problems. There were several teachers and helpers in the class. When they heard that Amanda was visiting Mindy's class, they asked if she would visit their class also.

As Amanda came into the class, the teacher told her that one particular child was extremely uncomfortable being touched, so please do not go near her. Amanda obliged and kept a respectful distance from the child, waving to her instead.

However, the child kept coming closer and closer to Amanda until *she* was touching Amanda! She never said a word, but seemed to like the feel of Amanda's heart and her fur. She stood there touching Amanda for several minutes!

In a separate class of autistic children, as Amanda was leaving the classroom, she inadvertently forgot to hug one of the teachers. A little boy tugged on Amanda's costume and repeatedly begged her, "Hug her! Hug her!" pointing to his teacher who had not received an Amanda hug. Amanda turned around and realized that she had hugged the other teachers in the class, but had missed his teacher. The teacher looked at Amanda with tears in her eyes and said, "Amanda, you have no way of knowing this, but Christopher has never put two words together before!" What a profound moment that was!

Mindy's Drawing

Mindy also knew *when* she was going to die. She loved to draw rainbows – they were her signature drawings and were always the same. Each of Mindy's rainbows contained seven colors and the colors were always drawn in the same sequence. First was the color red, followed by yellow, green, purple, orange, blue, and pink.

One day, Mindy sat down to draw her father a rainbow for his birthday, which was still a few weeks away. It was a beautiful rainbow but it was different than all the others. This rainbow contained only six colors instead of the usual seven. There was one color missing. It was the color pink - a color that is traditionally symbolic of little girls.

Mindy knew that she would not live to see her father's birthday, so she omitted the color pink from her rainbow. She also wrote these words on her final rainbow: Behind every dark cloud there's a rainbow.

Mindy died shortly after drawing her final rainbow and before her father's birthday.

Mindy receiving a stuffed panda from Amanda

Chapter 5
Brief Encounters
Lasting Impressions

Children with life-threatening illnesses had a way of wiggling their way deep into Amanda's heart, whether she saw them once or repeatedly over several months. This chapter is about one-time visits and the lasting impressions the children made.

Brady

"All I know is Heaven is BEAUTIFUL!" Brady, age thirteen

Brady was thirteen years old going on ninety in wisdom and courage! He loved pizza, and his favorite subject in school was history.

He had an inoperable tumor that was growing rapidly between his lung and his esophagus. The tumor caused him breathing problems which necessitated having an oxygen tank nearby.

Two years earlier, while swimming and diving, his knee became swollen. When his mother took him to the doctor, they discovered cancer. After two surgeries and chemotherapy, his leg was amputated. He received an encouraging letter from Ted Kennedy telling him that his own son had the same problem. The day Brady's tumor was diagnosed, a tornado came through his town and leveled his house. He also told Amanda that his mother had had polio and his uncle died because a doctor made a mistake.

Reflecting on all that had happened to him in his short life, Brady told Amanda, "Heaven's *GOT* to be better than this!" As they talked about Heaven, Brady looked forward to having no more surgeries, no more chemotherapy, and not ever being sick again. He said, "All I know is Heaven is BEAUTIFUL!"

The day Amanda arrived at his home, Brady was sitting on the davenport in the living room, an oxygen tank close by. The day before, he had breathing problems and needed oxygen, so it was very close in case he needed it.

He was very robust and, except for the obvious scar on his chest from the previous surgery and his missing leg, he actually looked relatively healthy. He coughed now and then, and it was apparent that breathing difficulties were imminent, but, generally speaking, he did not look as ill as he was. Yet, his mother told Amanda that she had been certain that he was going to die yesterday and was surprised that he was still alive today.

The doctors had told her that it was no longer a matter of months but rather days before he died. His brother who was in the service was granted an emergency leave and was due home that day. He would stay until the end.

While Amanda was in the room with him, Brady began to spit up, sort of like the dry heaves. His mother immediately got up to help him. Brady was ever so gentle and almost protective of her. He was very sensitive to her fears and tried to reassure her that it was nothing for her to be concerned about – that it was probably simply because he had had too much water to drink.

Amanda and Brady sat across from one another just soaking each other in. He was such an incredible young man, wise beyond his years. Brady talked about dying. "I'm not afraid to die, Amanda. Don't get me wrong, I'm in no hurry to die, but I figure when it comes, it comes. And whenever it comes, it's okay with me. We're all going to die sometime, you know. Heck, Amanda, you could croak on your way home, today!"

Brady died just a few days later. He made a very lasting impression on Amanda!

Brady and Amanda share a hug

Shani

"Sometimes you feel like crying because your mommy is so sad." Shani, age nine

Shani was nine years old and very close to death when Amanda first learned about her. She planned to visit Shani on her tenth birthday the following week, but the date of their visit was moved up when Shani was brought to the hospital emergency room by ambulance three days before her birthday. Shani was admitted to the hospital that day and never left. Amanda saw her only three times before she died.

Her mother called Amanda and asked her to come to the hospital instead of her home so they could celebrate Shani's birthday in Room 523. Amanda arrived carrying a birthday balloon and a soft, cuddly, stuffed panda bear for a birthday gift.

Shani seemed mesmerized by Amanda. Even though there were many friends, relatives, and hospital staff present while everyone sang Happy Birthday to Shani, she immediately focused on Amanda, and the two of them quickly became oblivious to all the other people in the room. It was almost as if they were the only two people present in Room 523. Their attention was totally on each other.

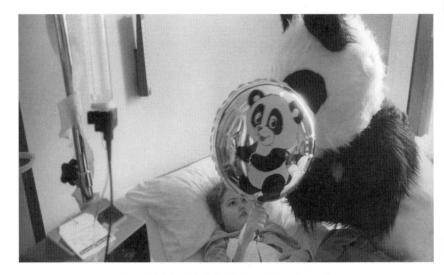

Shani with her birthday balloon from Amanda

Shani falling asleep in Amanda's arms

Shani asked Amanda what her favorite color was and was delighted to learn that it was lavender, the same as hers. Shani told Amanda that she had lost her tooth and was going to put it under her pillow and hoped the Tooth Fairy would find it in the hospital. They talked about lots of things and they hugged as Amanda promised she would return to see her again very soon.

On Amanda's second visit to Shani, her mother shared how angry Shani would often get with her and with the hospital chaplain. She said that whenever the chaplain would visit her, Shani would tell him to get out and would throw things at him. She also used very strong language filled with words that were certainly not very becoming of a young lady of ten. Sometimes, she would do the same thing to her mother.

Amanda explained that Shani did this because she knew that both of them would never leave her. After all, one was her mother who would love her forever, and the other represented God, who would never give up on her, no matter what. So Shani could be herself with both of them and let her anger fly, knowing that neither of them would ever abandon her.

Shani's relationship with Amanda was a much calmer one. She loved Amanda and Amanda loved her unconditionally. Their second visit was more of the same. They talked a lot and were very comfortable in each other's presence. They simply enjoyed getting to know more about each other.

Amanda's final visit to Shani was a very different story. The hospital chaplain called Amanda on Sunday evening and told her he didn't think Shani would live much longer. The end was very near, and if she wanted to see Shani again, she shouldn't delay.

It was 9:00 P.M. on that Sunday as Amanda rushed to the hospital and knocked on the door to Shani's room. The door was nearly closed, and, as she opened it, she asked Shani if she would like to have some company. Shani said yes, but her usual smile was gone. She was clearly in a lot of pain.

Her little stuffed panda bear was sitting on a bookshelf on the other side of the room, out of her reach. Amanda asked Shani if she would like her to get it for her, since it looked awfully lonely sitting by itself so far away. Shani told her that Amanda could get it and put it in her bed with her. Amanda liked that idea because the hospital bed looked way too large for Shani's little body. Having the bear in there would not make it look so big.

Amanda pulled up a chair and sat down beside her bed. Since it was hard for Shani to talk, Amanda said, "You know, Shani, we don't have to talk if you don't feel like it. Why don't I just sit here beside you, and we can let our hearts do the talking. My heart knows you love me and your heart knows I love you. So, we can just sit here and let our hearts talk to each other without having to say any words."

Amanda held Shani's hand and just sat beside her. In the silence of the night, two friends were very present to one another without having to say any words.

Pretty soon, Shani spoke, "Sometimes, you don't feel like talking because you feel like crying."

"And what makes you feel like crying, Shani?" Amanda asked gently.

"Sometimes you feel like crying because your mommy is so sad," she answered. "And sometimes you just wish everyone could be happy again the way things used to be. I know I will be going to Heaven soon and I will be okay. And I won't hurt anymore and that will make me very happy. But I think my mommy will be sad for a long time."

"Your mommy will miss you a lot, Shani. And she will be sad, too. But she will also be happy knowing that you are happy and will not be in pain ever again."

Amanda stayed with Shani until she fell asleep. Her final memory of Shani is seeing her snuggled up to her panda, sleeping peacefully. Shani died the very next day.

Darcie and Annie

Darcie and Annie were beautiful little girls who were best friends and lived in the same town, seventy miles from Des Moines. Darcie was six and had a congenital heart disorder, and Annie was three years old.

Amanda heard about them and visited them on a very hot summer day in June. She brought each of them a little stuffed panda bear with a heart just like Amanda's.

Annie's bear became her constant companion and went everywhere with her. When Annie was hospitalized, the bear was hospitalized, too! When she needed an IV tube in her arm, she asked to have her panda's arm hooked up to an IV, also.

Though Amanda only saw them one time, she would write them letters and send gifts in the mail. One time she sent Darcie an Amanda the Panda T-shirt and told her that she was the only little girl in her town who had one.

Darcie's mom wrote to Amanda and told her that as soon as Darcie heard that she was the only one in town with an Amanda the Panda T-shirt, she wore it *ALL THE TIME*; it was even hard to get it off of her to wash it.

Darcie died at the hospital late one night. Her parents were with her and stayed with her after she died for as long as they could. They held her in their arms and just hated to leave her. Eventually, there was nothing more they could do or say and Darcie's parents went home, brokenhearted.

The funeral director was called and arrived at the hospital shortly after her parents had left. He gently wrapped Darcie's body in her favorite blanket and took her to his funeral home. The hour was late; it was well past midnight when he got home.

He wondered if her parents were still up or if they had already gone to bed. Knowing that they would not get much sleep that night anyway, he called them.

They were, indeed, up and when they answered the phone, he identified himself and told them not to worry about their little girl. He said, "Your daughter is beautiful and she is safe with me. I'm a daddy, too, and will take very good care of her. In the morning when you are ready, come by the funeral home and we will make all the necessary arrangements. In the meantime, I just want you to know that she is with her favorite blanket and her panda bear." What a caring, compassionate funeral director he was!

Annie and Darcie were such close friends that, shortly after Darcie died, Annie's health started failing the very next day. Annie was playing with a tape recorder in the living room and recorded the following message, "One plus one is two. Zero plus zero is zero."

When Annie's mother played back the message, she discovered that Annie was actually talking about Darcie and how there once were two special friends. Then one died, leaving the other alone. Soon, the second one would die, which left both mothers with no more little girls!

A short time later, Annie was hospitalized for a week and never recovered. She died soon after her friend. The only consolation these young mothers had was that their precious daughters were together forever.

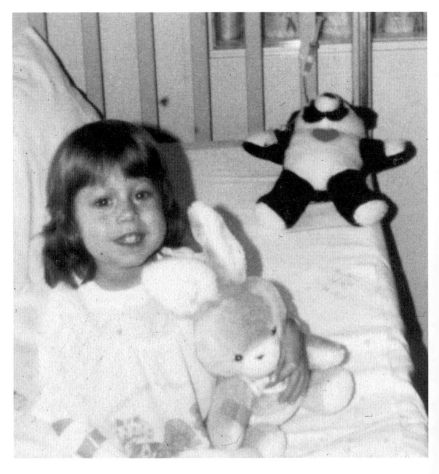

Annie and her panda bear in the hospital – an IV in both of them

Chapter 6
Tara

"I love you, Mom." *Tara, age eleven*

Tara was five years old when Amanda first stopped by her house to visit. She had a debilitating muscular disease that left her a captive of her own body. Her legs would not walk and her arms would not move. In the beginning she could say a few words, very slowly, but soon lost that ability also.

Tara could walk until she was three; then she became unable to do so and was confined to a wheelchair for the rest of her life. Amanda became her faithful companion for six years.

Unfortunately, many people do not take the time to get to know those who are different from them in some way. They miss out on so much by not making the effort to get to know them. Worse yet, they may think that people who cannot talk have nothing to say or have no personality. Nothing could be farther from the truth!

Eloquent In The Language Of Love

Tara had an incredible spirit and a smile that would light up the world. Although Tara couldn't speak with her voice, she was a master at communicating her moods and desires. Whenever Amanda would come to visit her, Tara would literally *squeal* with delight. Her entire being expressed her joy. There was no mistaking how happy she was, giving the same response at the mere mention of her brother's name. She loved her brother Bradley so much that all you had to do was mention his name and her entire face would break out into one huge smile. They always laughed, played, and even cried together.

One time, while Tara was siting in her wheelchair on a hot, summer day, Bradley was entertaining her. He was bouncing around only in shorts and dancing for her, and they were both giggling hilariously. Bradley threw his arms wide open and fell back to sit on the floor, but unfortunately miscalculated and sat in his mother's big barrel cactus instead. He started to scream and Tara started to cry. Their mother didn't know which child to save first - to take the spines out of Bradley or to try to keep Tara from choking on her tears!

Tara's mother took exceptional care of her. A little girl through and through, she was never a tomboy. She loved wearing long lacy dresses, ponytails and barrettes, nail polish, makeup, and perfume.

Her long, beautiful blond hair was always combed and put up in two ponytails. She usually wore lavender ponytail holders and ribbons in her hair. Her fingernails were painted and she always looked pretty. If it were up to Tara, her dresses and blouses and slacks would have been lavender, also. She loved the color! Some believe that lavender is a spiritual color, which would be very appropriate because Tara had a very special gift. She had the ability to lift the spirits of everyone who came in contact with her, making them immediately fall in love with her. Tara was beautiful inside and out, and always a joy to visit.

She gave so much love that people were unafraid to talk to or touch a disabled person. The understanding she passed on to people who were never exposed to disabilities was priceless.

Tara had a real zest for life and a contagious smile. She loved to have her picture taken – especially with Amanda. She appeared in many newspaper and magazine articles with Amanda and was featured on several television segments with her, too.

Bradley opening the door for Amanda

Tara snuggled in Amanda's arms

Amanda would often make up songs and sing Tara to sleep when she was restless and fighting for her life; Amanda never sang out loud for anyone but Tara. She would make up songs about the two of them, and at one point in the song, Tara would giggle. She always knew when that part was coming, even when she appeared to be unconscious. Whenever she was extremely restless or in distress, Amanda would sing this song to calm her. Always, at Tara's favorite spot, she would smile or giggle.

Amanda loved holding Tara in her arms and rocking her in her favorite rocking chair; she would write her poems and stay all night with her in the hospital. One of the poems Amanda wrote for Tara toward the end of her life was entitled, "Thank You, Dear Tara." Her mother asked JoAnn to read it at Tara's funeral.

Tara was often on the brink of death and then would rally again. One of her mother's favorite memories was during one of those times that she thought her precious little girl was going to die at any moment.

Her mother broke down in front of her telling her how sad she was that Tara was going through all of this and how much she loved her. Tara was pale, barely breathing, had pneumonia, and was on oxygen. Still, she mustered up all the strength she had and pulled a long forgotten voice from somewhere deep within and said, "I love you, Mom."

Tara was totally wiped out for the rest of the night. Her mother had not heard her voice for over three years and will always remember and treasure that moment.

That was a perfect example of Tara. She was suffering so much, yet trying to comfort others.

Tara died peacefully in her mother's arms in the wee hours of the morning. Close by was her faithful friend of six years, Amanda the Panda.

Thank You, Dear Tara

It seems like only yesterday when you were five
And I came sauntering up your drive
Bearing gifts and hugs galore
I stood excitedly at your door

I wondered who this Tara and Bradley were
I fell deeply in love with both of them, that's for sure
Do you remember, Tara, that first day
When I came in and we started to play?

You looked so pretty with your hair combed just right
With ponytails and barrettes and your nails painted bright
You were dressed in your favorite color, with your ears pierced, too
Your mother always took such good care of you

You squealed with delight as we kissed, panda style
Rubbing our noses together and holding each other close for a while
We played together and Brad was nearby
And when I left, you waved me goodbye
Over the years, your body slowed down
But on your face there was barely a frown
In spite of the fact that your voice would not speak
Your legs would not walk and your body grew weak

Your charm was intact and you flirted with EVERYONE
Special male nurses, doctors, visitors, and all who would come
Your playfulness and sense of humor were not to be outdone
As evidenced by the presence of your loaded squirt gun

You smiled and you loved and were patient beyond measure
Tara, I'll love you forever and your gifts I will treasure
The gift of your smile was so special to me
It was a visible sign for all to see

The beautiful being held captive, in part
The depths of your spirit – the love in your heart
Be free and at peace to soar high above
Thank you, dear Tara, for the gift of your love!

Tara looking at a photo of Amanda holding her

Chapter 7
DeeDee

"Amanda, I'm going to hide you in the cloak closet and then, when it is time for show and tell, I will come and get you!" DeeDee, age seven

Oftentimes, children in classrooms and on school playgrounds can be quite cruel to their classmates when they perceive them as different in some way. It doesn't matter what it is that makes them stand out. They make fun of them for a multitude of reasons, none of them ever justified.

One of Amanda's early missions was to go into the schools and teach children to care about one another, to support one another, and to include all children in their circle of friends. Going into the schools was one of Amanda's favorite things to do.

One day in late fall while Amanda was making hospital rounds, she met a beautiful little girl named DeeDee who had recently been diagnosed with cancer and was just beginning to lose her beautiful, long, blond hair. Even though DeeDee was seven years old and had never had her hair cut, it was now coming out in clumps. She still had three more weeks of treatments, and then it would be time for Christmas break before she could return to school. By then, she would certainly be completely bald. Her mother was concerned about how her classmates would treat DeeDee when she went back to school for the first time with no hair. She knew that the first day back could be potentially difficult for DeeDee and for everyone if it didn't go well. It could negatively affect her entire attitude toward school, which, until now, had been very positive.

DeeDee's mother was aware that Amanda often accompanied children back to school after hair loss, and she thought that would be the perfect solution. So she asked Amanda if she would like to accompany DeeDee to school after the holidays. It would be DeeDee's first time back since she was diagnosed with cancer in October.

DeeDee's Plan

Amanda immediately wrote down the date on her calendar and then asked DeeDee if she had any specific thoughts as to how this would happen. Amanda asked DeeDee if she wanted her to meet her at school at the principal's office first thing in the morning, or if she wanted Amanda to come to her home and they would go to school together, or exactly how she would like for this to happen.

DeeDee said, "Oh no, Amanda, I don't want you to wait for me at school in the principal's office or to come to my house and walk me to school. I live too far away from school to walk. I have a better plan!"

DeeDee was now *really* getting excited! "I am going to put you in the cloak closet so no one will see you, and then I will come and get you for show and tell."

Amanda was happy to see her excitement and loved it that she had a plan. So, off she went on the appointed day, and DeeDee quickly put her in the cloak closet to await the time that she would come and get her.

JoAnn had told Amanda that show and tell time is usually first thing in the morning, so Amanda was not worried. She happily let DeeDee put her in the cloak closet at 8:45 A.M. Before long, it was 9:15 A.M., and Amanda was certain that DeeDee would be coming to get her very soon. Well, she soon found out that show and tell may have been first thing in the morning when JoAnn went to school, but that's not the way it was at DeeDee's school!

Show and tell time was just before lunch at DeeDee's school! Amanda thought she would *die or faint* in that very small, confined cloak closet. There was no ventilation, and it was crowded with coats, hats, mittens, boots, and lunch boxes. Furthermore, it was January, so Amanda was still wearing her long-haired coat. It was getting mighty hot in there! She waited for DeeDee for two and a half hours!

Finally, just before lunch DeeDee came to get her! She took her by the hand and introduced her to her entire class. "This is my very best friend, Amanda the Panda," she said.

Amanda replied, "And this is my very best friend, DeeDee."

For the next half hour Amanda talked about friendship and

what it means to be a friend. The children shared how friends make you feel and how they never laugh at you if you give the wrong answer or make fun of you if you look different or are new to the class. They talked about how you can be yourself with your friends, and that they will like you and stand by you, no matter what.

Amanda talked about how it doesn't matter what you look like on the outside – whether you have big feet, large ears, glasses, or no hair – because the outside is just your shell. What really matters is who you are on the inside and how much love you have for others. Amanda asked the children how many of them had a best friend in the class. Several hands went up. She asked how many would like to *be* a best friend to someone who might not have one. Everyone raised their hand. Amanda then asked the teacher to write down the names of the children who would like to be someone's friend, and post it in a prominent place in the classroom where everyone could see it every day. That way, whenever anyone needed a friend, all they had to do was go to the poster and choose a name from the list.

Amanda was so proud of this class! She knew that DeeDee would not have any problems; they would stick by her through thick and thin because that's what friends do. In this class, DeeDee had lots of friends.

Amanda gave each child a pencil with her picture on it so they could remember her and what they had talked about. Then everyone lined up to receive a great big bear hug before they went to lunch.

DeeDee playing in the sand at Camp-A-Panda

Chapter 8
Michael

"Amanda, how come you gots a zipper?" Michael, age three

There is good news! Not all children with cancer die. Michael is another success story. Amanda met him on the very day he was diagnosed, when he was three years old. She was making hospital rounds and stopped in to see the little boy everyone was talking about with the curly, fire-engine red hair. His parents were standing outside his room, visibly upset and heartbroken. She stopped to talk with them, and they introduced her to their very precious child.

Michael and Amanda sort of grew up together. He was three and she was two. However, in panda years, that is much, much older. Michael was in his hospital bed with an IV hooked up to his arm. He was standing in the bed and couldn't wait to put his arms around the giant panda who sauntered into his room. He wasn't a bit afraid. They hugged immediately and a long-lasting love affair began. It has lasted more than two decades, and it has been interesting to watch their relationship change as Michael has grown developmentally.

From the beginning, Amanda would visit him in the hospital and in his home. She would visit in the fall, in the winter, in the spring, and in the summer. She was with him during relapses and remissions. The remissions were great celebrations, and the relapses were heart wrenching for everyone.

Michael loved to have Amanda come to his home. On the days she would visit, he would always be watching out the window, waiting for her to walk up the sidewalk and stop at his front door. Before she could ring the doorbell, he would fling open the door as wide as he could so that Amanda could get through. Once inside, he would follow her to the rocking chair, wait for her to sit down, and then climb onto her lap.

The Power Of Observation

As winter turned to spring, Amanda's long-haired winter coat was much too hot for springtime temperatures in Iowa, so she changed to a short-haired costume. The first time Michael saw her in her new costume, he looked perplexed. He looked up and down at her repeatedly and finally said, "Amanda, did you gets a haircut?"

Later that same day, he noticed the zipper on her new costume. "Amanda," he said, "how come you gots a zipper?" Amanda wasn't sure how to respond to that question, so she said a quick prayer for inspiration and said, "Michael, honey, we *all* have a zipper. You have one, too." Michael looked down at his pants, noticed his own zipper and simply and matter-of-factly, said, "Oh." That seemed to make perfect sense to him.

Making Memories

Michael would share the poems he learned in school with Amanda, along with other very important things he would learn. Once, he wanted to show Amanda how he could blow a big bubble with his bubble gum. Amanda was a bit nervous, but he was so very proud of this newly developed skill. As he sat on Amanda's lap and started to blow the biggest bubble ever, it popped and got all over Amanda's furry hair and nose. "Oops!" he said. "I still need to practice some." Then he giggled with delight as he tried his best to remove the bubble gum from her nose and fur.

Michael loved having his picture taken with Amanda and appeared in numerous local and national television interviews with her. He was also featured with Amanda in *LIFE* magazine in October of 1985.

Youngest Camper At Camp-A-Panda

In 1984, Amanda created the first camp in Iowa for children eight to eighteen years of age who were living with cancer. Michael was only five years old at the time. He heard about camp and emphatically informed his doctor that he would be going to Camp-A-Panda.

His doctor, very logically, said, "Michael, you can't go to Camp-A-Panda because you are only five years old and you must be eight to attend camp."

Undaunted, Michael said, "Huh uh! I know Amanda the Panda and I am going to call her up." He called Amanda on the telephone and said, "Amanda, I am coming to your camp! Oops. I mean, uh, I'm supposed to ask first. Can I come to your camp even if I am only five? Dr. Elliott says I have to be eight." "Well, Michael, Dr. Elliott is right; everyone will be at least eight years old," replied Amanda. "But you can come for a few days, and when you get homesick, I will take you home."

"No, Amanda!" said Michael. "I want to come for the whole week. I want to be with you!"

"Okay, Michael, you come and stay as long as you wish. I will be waiting for you at camp."

Michael came to camp armed with his little Brownie camera with a huge viewfinder. Whether or not it had film in it, no one knew. Michael didn't care. He took pictures of everything and everyone. He even took pictures of people taking pictures of him. Michael had the week of a lifetime!

One evening after the campfire, he and Amanda were walking back to his cabin together, hand in hand, when Michael said, "Do you gots anything to eat around here this time of night, Amanda?"

"Sure, Michael, let's go find a snack in the kitchen. I know we have some raisins." (Amanda was thinking healthy snacks rather than sugar snacks at 9:00 P.M.)

"Nope, don't like raisins," he said, "they make me poop!"

Michael was having a blast. Even though he was three years younger than the youngest campers, he stayed the entire week and became friends with everyone. He was the youngest child at camp and became the darling of the camp, with his fire-engine red hair and his Brownie camera, with or without film in it, hanging around his neck.

Michael and Karen, his counselor, in a hot air balloon at Camp-A-Panda

When camp was over, everyone received a camper list with the names, addresses, and phone numbers of everyone in camp so that they could keep in touch with one another if they so desired.

Michael went home and soon found himself thinking about and missing his new camp friends. One day, he began calling them. He began at the top of the alphabet and started calling all his new friends from Camp-A-Panda. He got half way through the alphabet before the phone bill arrived. Michael knew nothing about long distance telephone rates; he just knew that he had made lots of friends and thought it would be nice to talk to them again.

When the first phone bill arrived and Michael's mom opened it, she was shocked at all the long distance charges on it. Immediately, she went to her husband and asked him who in the world he had been calling. He looked at the phone bill and said, "Those are not my calls! I don't recognize a single phone number and they are all over the state! Who have *you* been calling?"

Michael, overhearing this "discussion," excitedly ran in from the other room and announced that those were *HIS* calls to some of his friends from Camp-A-Panda. He was so proud!

Growing Older

As Michael got older, his feelings for Amanda became conflicted. He loved Amanda with his whole heart, but, as a preteen soon to be a teenager, it was not too cool to be seen with a bear. This was entirely new for Amanda, too.

Amanda asked JoAnn to step in. JoAnn had come to know Michael quite well over the years through Amanda and was happy to do so. Even though Michael had suspected for a few years that JoAnn was Amanda, he treated both of them very differently.

For Christmas, JoAnn gave Michael a calendar with a panda design on it. On each month, a specific day was set aside for the two of them to have a "date." Michael could choose anything he wanted to do. On some dates, he and JoAnn would go out for pizza or ice cream; other times, they went to the botanical center or the zoo or a movie. In that way, they could still be a part of each other's lives, and he could share what was going on in his life at school or at home.

When he graduated from high school, JoAnn was invited to his graduation party. Through the years, he would send her Christmas cards so she could keep up with his jobs and other interests. He has since moved out of town, but when he comes back to visit his grandmother at Christmastime, they get together in person or by phone to remember old times. One thing is certain, Michael has never forgotten Amanda and Amanda has never forgotten Michael - he has a special place in her heart.

Michael proudly receiving his medal at Camp-A-Panda

Michael with another young friend at Camp-A-Panda

Chapter 9
Camp-A-Panda
A Camp For Children With Cancer

"Should you shield the canyons from the windstorms, you would not see the beauty of their carvings." Elisabeth Kubler-Ross

Amanda the Panda was created in 1980. Very quickly, another dream surfaced. As Amanda met and fell in love with children living with cancer, she realized that they were children first, and cancer patients second. Children with cancer have the same longings as other children their age. They, too, want to go to summer camp for a week where they can ride horses, go swimming, sit around a campfire and tell stories, and do all the things "normal" kids get to do at camp.

However, many "regular" summer camp programs are not so welcoming to children with cancer because they don't feel they can accommodate their medical needs. They are also not sure that children with cancer can do all the things that other children can do.

It took Amanda three years to raise the money to make her dream come true – to have a summer camp exclusively for children with cancer. It would be called Camp-A-Panda, and would be the week of a lifetime. All children with cancer in Iowa would be welcome. Children who were newly diagnosed were as welcome as those in remission. Those who had relapsed or had no hair or were missing limbs were all welcome at Camp-A-Panda.

At Camp-A-Panda, everyone understood what it was like to have cancer. No one would laugh or make fun of anyone. No child would have to wear a wig or be ashamed of how their cancer made them different from the kids at school.

Teens in remission would be a sign of hope for young children newly diagnosed; the young ones could look at the older kids and say, "YES! I can live to be their age, too!" Children in wheelchairs

Mark in wheelchair fishing at Camp-A-Panda

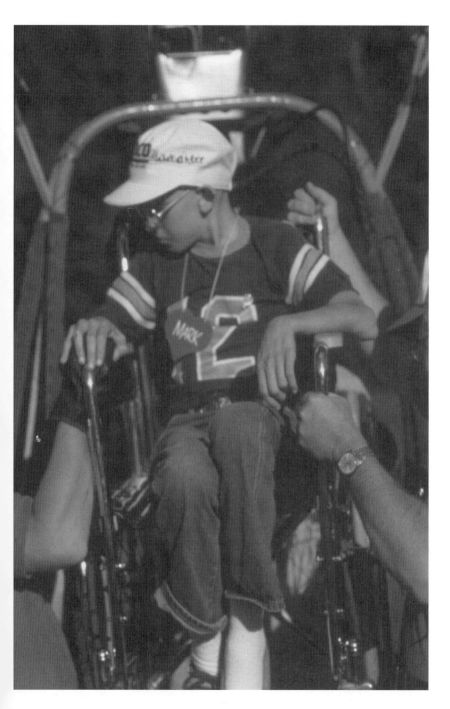

Mark going for a hot air balloon ride

could ride in a hot air balloon, go fishing, and do what everyone else was doing. They wouldn't be limited by their wheelchairs in any way.

The children would have their own doctors and nurses at camp, so their medical protocols would be followed. They could get all of their medicines at camp, and, best of all, they could play miniature golf with their doctors and nurses or go horseback riding with them. They could see their medical staff in a totally different light, and vice-versa.

Everyday there would be lots of surprises and a different theme. There would be clowns, musicians, horseback riding, arts and crafts, hot air balloon rides, swimming, archery, hiking, fishing, cabin skits, and a big dance at the end of the week. For some children, this was their first dance.

Counselors danced with the kids, kids danced with their doctors and nurses, and some of the kids asked other kids to be their "date" for the dance. For some, this was their first date. Everyone had a good time, and their self-esteem skyrocketed. They tried things they never knew they could do. They made lots of friends and they felt normal, not different.

The first year, 1984, Amanda was expecting twenty or thirty children with cancer to come to camp. Instead, she got sixty-eight! The second year, the number grew to eighty-seven; the third year, one hundred and two; and the fourth year, one hundred eighteen children attended Camp-A-Panda! Today, the camp continues under the name The Heart Connection.

Cabin Skits

At Camp-A-Panda, each of the cabins were invited to present a cabin skit to the entire camp on Friday evening. The kids would plan and practice their skits for days. There were props, a microphone, and a stage. Anything they might need was provided for them. They came up with some elaborate skits. Some were funny. Others showcased nearly professional talent and musical ability. But the cabin skit that stands out in everyone's memory is the Shagbark Cabin skit.

Shagbark cabin housed the teenagers. They asked for

permission to be the last skit of the evening, the grand finale. Permission was granted. As their cabin name was called, they all came forward.

There was a narrator who read the script they had written, and the other teen campers acted out the various parts. The girl who played the part of "Gladys" was Kelisa, a teenager who did not have a single strand of hair on her head. When she arrived at camp, she wore a wig and a prosthesis for her right leg. By the end of the first day, she took off her wig and never wore it again the rest of the week. Kelisa was absolutely *stunningly* beautiful!

Their skit is presented here in its entirety, including the postscript they wrote.

Mark with Amanda at Camp-A-Panda

Shagbark Campers' Skit

Once upon a time there was a girl named Gladys. One fine morning she woke up feeling rather badly, so her mother took her to see the doctor. His name was Dr. Hoover. Dr. Hoover ran some tests on Gladys and told her and her family that she had an illness which required some special treatments. The treatments were called chemotherapy and radiation therapy.

Soon afterwards, Gladys started going to the hospital to have her chemotherapy treatments. She also received radiation therapy treatments. Gladys was told she may lose some or all of her hair, but for some reason, she never really gave it much thought . . . until one day, Gladys woke up, got out of bed, and looked at herself in a mirror. Gladys was shocked at what she saw staring back at her. There was a girl who looked just like Gladys, except all of her hair was gone!

Gladys felt weird and funny at school with her friends and even uncomfortable with her own family members. All Gladys could see when she looked in the mirror was the girl with no hair. She couldn't see the wonderful person living inside her.

Then one day she met Amanda the Panda who changed her life forever. First, Amanda introduced her to other children who had similar illnesses and problems coping with them. Amanda helped Gladys see that it isn't what you see on the outside of a person that makes them special; it's getting to know the person on the inside and finding out just how wonderful they really are. Beauty is only skin deep, and the true beauty of a person lies deep within themselves.

Gladys now understands that she, too, is a beautiful person, even if she doesn't have any of her own hair.

Now, when Gladys looks in the mirror she no longer sees the frightened and lonely child she once was, but sees a wonderful, cheerful, and happy young girl with many friends and dreams for her future. The End. (Then they added the following postscript.)

The moral of the story is: It doesn't matter how your illness affects you, you are still the same person on the inside. Beauty isn't only on the outside of a person. Live every day to its fullest and be all you can be! Don't be afraid to go out and let everybody know just how wonderful you really are!

Kelisa, a true champion, receiving her medal at Camp-A-Panda

Chapter 10
Camp Amanda
A Camp For Those Who Mourn

"Blessed are they who weep and mourn, for they shall be comforted." Beatitudes

Whenever one of Amanda's special friends died, JoAnn would go to their funeral rather than Amanda. It would have been disruptive and rather difficult for a seven-foot panda bear to blend in with the mourners at a church service. The focus at the church rightfully belonged to celebrating the child's life and to saying good-bye.

A month or so after the funeral, JoAnn would return to take the child's mother and father to lunch to be of support to them and to see how they were doing. During those lunches, parents often shared their concerns about how their other children were doing and how their sibling's death affected them.

Frequently, parents asked JoAnn if Amanda would return to their home for one more visit to their other children who were now grieving the death of their sibling, as well as the loss of Amanda's visits.

Amanda was eager to see her little friends again and loved those follow-up visits. The children were always honest and open about sharing their thoughts and feelings about their sibling's death with Amanda. They talked about the funeral and what it was like now that their brother or sister had died. They shared how their lives had changed and what they missed. They talked about what they remembered most and how their role in the family had changed. They talked about their sadness and regrets.

When Amanda asked them if they would share with their parents what they had shared with her, every single child answered the same way. *Every* child without hesitation answered with an emphatic NO.

They told Amanda that their mother and father were sad

enough now that their sibling had died. If they shared their own feelings with them, it would make their parents even sadder. They couldn't bear to do that, so they kept their feelings to themselves and cried in their beds at night privately.

These children were *protecting* their parents – the very ones who wanted to help them the most. The parents were grieving the same death and, oftentimes, had little emotional energy left to help their children. Sometimes, it took all their energy and strength to just get up in the mornings. Understandably, the death of a child is shattering to a parent! There is no pain like it.

An Unmet Need Fulfilled

JoAnn asked herself, "Where do children go to share their feelings of grief if they are choosing not to share them with their parents?" The answer was that there was no place. They were keeping all these feelings to themselves. In 1982, in Iowa, there was no place for children to go to "dump" these feelings on people they didn't feel they needed to protect. Unfortunately, in many states today that is still the case.

Seeing the great need that existed for a place where grieving children could talk openly and freely about their experience, JoAnn created Camp Amanda, a weekend camp exclusively for children whose siblings had died. She gathered all of Amanda's friends whose brother or sister had died and invited them to come to a camp just for them.

No parents were allowed at Camp Amanda, so the children could speak freely and not feel the need to protect anyone.

It was an incredibly successful camp. The children were able to open up and get some of their sadness out so they could make room inside for happiness.

An interesting phenomenon occurred before the first year ended. Parents approached JoAnn with news that their spouse died, wanting to know if their children could come to Camp Amanda. Others told her that their parent had died and that their children had a very close relationship with their grandparent, so could *they* come to this camp? Teens whose boyfriends or girlfriends were killed in car accidents asked if they could come to Amanda's camp. The answer to all these questions was a resounding, "YES! EVERYONE IS WELCOME!"

Over and over, as parents came to pick up their children at the end of camp they would say, "Thank you, thank you, thank you! You have given us our old Jimmy back. The sparkle is back in his eyes that we haven't seen since his father's death. We can see that something significant happened here this weekend. Would you ever consider doing something like this for us adults?"

Today, there are three camps each year for children and teens and, during the same weekend, three separate camps for adults, some of whom are parents of the children who come to camp. The adult camp is completely separate from the children's camp, and everyone is reunited at the closing ceremony on Sunday. Adults do not have to have a child at camp to be able to participate.

Adult campers at Camp Amanda

Camp Amanda is now for anyone dealing with the death of someone they love who has died through accident, illness, suicide, or homicide. To date, thousands of grieving children and families in every county in Iowa, plus twenty-three other states, have attended Camp Amanda.

Although there are several components at camp designed to facilitate healing, a high priority is placed on having fun. The following poem reflects the philosophy of Camp Amanda and the work done with bereaved children.

> *I tried to teach my child with books*
> *and all I got were puzzled looks.*
> *I tried to teach my child with words,*
> *they passed him by, oft unheard.*
> *Then into my hand he put the key;*
> *"Come," he said, "and play with me."*

Grieving children and adults need to know that it is just as important to be able to laugh and play and have fun again, as it is to be able to cry when they are feeling sad. Doing so is not being disrespectful to the memory of the person who died.

At Camp Amanda, bereaved children and families are able to meet others their age who also have experienced a death in their family. They learn from one another that the feelings they are experiencing are normal, and they are not the only ones who feel this way. They feel much less isolated, alone, and different, no matter what their circumstances. Camp Amanda creates a safe environment where unconditional love abounds. Children and teens learn that both tears and laughter are important in the grieving process. They are not so much taught these things as they are modeled for them. Miracles happen everyday at Camp Amanda. It is truly holy ground!

Camp Amanda cooks: Ron, Gene, Kathy, Robin and Sandie

Teens at Camp Amanda

A Tragic Accident

One day a mother called Amanda the Panda's office, desperation evident in her voice and a clear feeling of hopelessness at nowhere to turn in her small community near Des Moines.

She shared that she had three children and was recovering from cancer surgery. Her own mother died less than six months previously, but neither of these life-altering events was the subject of her call. Her concern was for her eleven-year-old son, Brian.

Brian was an active, athletically gifted, good-looking boy. He was an above average student with lots of friends and a lot going for him. He loved being outdoors and being with his family. His father and uncles took him fishing and hunting and played basketball with him every night. He made the all-star team in baseball. He idolized his favorite uncle who would go target practicing with him and taught him to fish. Life was good.

Then it happened. One day, one event, and Brian's life was turned upside down. Brian's father, uncles, and cousins had gone hunting on a beautiful, crisp, fall day. It was Brian's first real hunting experience and he was with his favorite uncle. He loved being with him and being outdoors.

Brian and his favorite uncle were behind a tree when they noticed a rabbit scurry out from the bushes. Brian quickly took aim, and as he fired his rifle, it bumped the trunk of the tree, misfired, and he accidentally shot and killed his uncle. In an instant, one life was ended and another was tragically transformed.

Brian blamed himself and no longer wanted to live. He became distant, not caring anymore about life, sports, school, friends, or family. His self-esteem plummeted.

On his first day back to school after the accident, classmates called him "killer" and "murderer." He got into fights, became hostile, and continually got into trouble with his teachers. His grades were on a downward spiral towards straight F's.

The family went to counseling, and the counselor recommended that they all attend Camp Amanda. Brian attended camp first, and the rest of his family came to a later camp.

When he arrived at camp, everyone's heart went out to him! All of the camp counselors took him under their wing. They were so tender and gentle with him. Even the other campers were kind and compassionate to him, for they knew firsthand the pain of living without someone they loved. No one at Camp Amanda called him names or got into fights with him. The other children asked Brian to play baseball with them.

Everyone saw what happened for what it was – a tragic accident. In this loving environment, slowly, he began to tell his story. Everyone cried. At Camp Amanda, the healing began.

At the end of camp, a list of staff and campers' names and addresses was given to every person to take home. Throughout the next several weeks and months, Brian received many notes and letters from his friends at camp – kids and adults alike. His mother said he kept them in a shoebox in a closet in his room. She said she could always tell when he was having a bad day at school. He would come home, slam the door, and go straight to his room. He would take his shoebox down from the shelf in his closet, sit on the floor, and read every letter he had received. Later, when he was ready, he would join the rest of the family. She said he was always in a better mood when he came down. She also said that after camp his grades began improving. He no longer had straight F's. He now had some B's and C's.

At Amanda the Panda's Christmas party that year, JoAnn made a point of telling Brian how proud she was of him and how far he had come in a few short months. He looked at her, smiled his impish grin, and said, "I'm still working on my math grade. It's a C+ now, but I know I can bring it up to a B soon."

Ashlin, our golden retriever, posing with campers

Big Pat, Little Pat

Michael Patrick was a six-year-old camper who really bonded with his twenty-three-year-old male counselor, Pat, who was over six feet tall with broad shoulders. Little Michael Patrick fell in love with Pat so much that he changed his own name from Michael Patrick to Patrick Michael. For the rest of camp, he wanted to be known as "Little Pat."

As Pat the counselor, who now became known as "Big Pat," lit his candle during the candlelight ceremony, he told everyone that his candle represented his grandfather. He shared that he really missed him and all the things they used to do. Then, Big Pat gently wiped away a tear.

Michael, who was sitting in Pat's lap during the candlelight ceremony, noticed Pat wiping away a tear. After the candlelight ceremony, the following dialogue took place.

Little Pat:	Pat, do **BIG** boys cry?
Big Pat:	Well, yeah, they cry sometimes.
Little Pat:	Pat, did **YOU** cry?
Big Pat	(a bit embarrassed) Well, yeah I cried.
Little Pat:	Good! 'Cause I cried, too!

Camp Amanda is a true balance of laughter and tears. The freedom to express one's true self exists at camp because no one makes fun of anyone, ever, at Camp Amanda! It is simply not allowed. Because a high priority is placed on having fun, the children always want to come back again. The camp evaluations are extremely positive.

Counselors Lisa, Mark, and Susan

Better Than Walt Disney World

Petey, an eight-year-old whose grandmother died, described his experience best in the following conversation with JoAnn on the last day of camp. It was Sunday morning when Petey approached JoAnn and said, "JoAnn, this camp was AWESOME! It was better than Walt Disney World! I can't wait to come to the next one! When is the next one?"

"Oh, Petey, honey, you can't come to the next one," JoAnn told him. "The reason you can't come again is that if we had allowed all the children from the last camp who wanted to come again to return, there wouldn't have been room for you at this camp. You can only come to Camp Amanda once, unless someone else in your family dies, and we sure hope that doesn't happen!"

Petey looked devastated, like someone had popped his balloon. He hung his head as he just stood there trying to absorb what JoAnn had told him. Then, all of a sudden, he perked up. It was as if the sun had come out again after a thunderstorm. He looked right at JoAnn and said, "My aunt's sick!" (JoAnn is pretty sure that she only had the flu!)

One little girl summed it up best when she said, "Before Camp Amanda, I felt sad, mad, and scared, but now I feel brand new."

Along with cookouts, games, relays, and tie-dyeing t-shirts, there are opportunities and activities designed to facilitate healing and to dispel any misconceptions that children may have.

Doctor Question and Answer Period

One component at Camp Amanda is a question and answer period with a doctor who answers medical questions that may still linger in children's minds. Our camp physician is a very warm and friendly person who likes kids and can answer questions on a child's level, using words they understand. Rarely do children have an opportunity to ask a doctor questions related to the death. The following story is an example of how profound this question and answer period can be.

Counselors Deb and Jan preparing camp for the children's arrival

Hannah's Story

Hannah was eighteen months old when her mother died of cancer. At the time of their mother's death, Hannah's two brothers were six and seven, and her sister was eight. Hannah's siblings and her father attended camp, but she had to wait until she turned six, the minimum age required for camp.

When Hannah turned six she attended Camp Amanda. At first she sat very quietly on the floor in her counselor's lap and listened attentively to the doctor answer the other children's questions. Slowly, timidly, her hand went up. "Doctor, what causes cancer?" she asked, in her tender little voice. He answered her question using simple terms that she could understand.

A few moments later, Hannah's other hand went up. A second time she asked, "Doctor, what causes cancer?" Again he answered her question.

She listened and paid very close attention to what he was saying, yet a *third* time she raised her hand and asked the very same question again, "Doctor, what causes cancer?"

At that point, her counselor understood the REAL question Hannah was trying so hard to ask, but simply didn't have the words to articulate. The counselor raised her hand and asked, "Doctor, if a woman gets cancer when she is pregnant and after the baby is born, the mother dies, is it the baby's fault that her mother died?"

That was it! That was the question Hannah was trying so desperately to ask, but just didn't know how. This crucial question had impacted her entire life!

The doctor told her that it was absolutely *NOT* the baby's fault that the mother died! With his answer he had finally put to rest the guilt that Hannah had carried all of her life. You could see that a huge weight had been lifted from Hannah's heart! Her whole being reflected it!

The next day, when her two brothers, her sister, and her father came to camp for the closing ceremony, Hannah ran right over to her brothers, put her hands on her hips, and said to them, "I did *NOT* kill Mommy! There was a doctor here last night and he said it was *NOT MY FAULT!*"

Dr. Dave answering children's questions at Camp Amanda

The Military Man

Another memorable camper was a middle-aged, military man who was the father of two teen-aged boys. He was just a few years away from full retirement from the service. His wife had died of cancer, and he was a very bitter man. Most of all, he was angry with God for not sparing his wife.

When he arrived at Camp Amanda, he said he was only there so his children could get the help they needed. He also announced that he and the boys would be leaving very early on Sunday morning because he had to be at his Air Force Base later that day.

After signing in, taking their gear to their cabins, and saying goodbye to his boys, he joined the other adults for the weekend.

At the adult camp he met other husbands whose wives had died, and he began to feel at home. As the weekend progressed, he shared his story. He told how his wife was a wonderful person and a dedicated mother. They had been looking forward to his retiring from the military, the boys growing up and going to college, and having the time to enjoy each other exclusively. They had dreams of traveling together and maybe even building a little A-frame cabin in the woods one day.

Then she got cancer and it ravaged her body. She was so sick for so long and got weaker and weaker by the day. She died way too soon! And all the dreams they had died with her. Now he was left to be both mother and father to the boys, and he wasn't sure how to do that. The boys needed their mother and her gentle ways. She was the spontaneous, fun parent; he was the disciplined, serious, military man. How could God do this to him and to his family? "I will never forgive you, God," he said over and over.

As he got to know the other campers and hear their stories, he knew he was not alone. He was among friends. They didn't judge him, they only accepted him.

He thought he had come to camp for the boys' benefit only; he soon realized, however, how much better he was feeling. The other campers were no longer strangers; they were people traveling on the same journey. Their stories were unique to them, but the feelings they expressed were familiar ones.

On Sunday morning he arose early before any of the other campers were awake, put on his military uniform, gathered his belongings, and got ready to go get his boys and head to the base.

Before he left, he did one more thing. He left a message for all to see when they woke up. He picked up a piece of chalk and on the blackboard in the retreat center he wrote in very large letters, "I forgive you, God."

The Candlelight Ceremony

Another camp activity designed to promote healing is the candlelight ceremony. It has become one of the most profound parts of the weekend and takes place on Saturday evening following the doctor question and answer period.

All of the children and their counselors sit in a circle on the floor and every person is given a red, cinnamon-scented candle in the shape of a teddy bear. The candles are made with love by a very special candle maker in Texas and donated to Camp Amanda by a wonderful woman who believes in the mission of camp. In fact, these special candles are no longer in production and are only made for Camp Amanda.

The candles all look alike as they are given to each child. But, soon, every child will personalize their own candle and make it intrinsically different from everyone else's. As they light their candle, they tell who it represents and then share a memory of that person. Some memories are funny, some are poignant, and all of them come from the heart. To sit among the children as they light their candles and share their memories is a profound privilege and a spiritual experience. The words sacred and holy immediately come to mind for God is truly present among his children. His presence is tangible!

There wasn't a dry eye in the place as one little boy lit his candle and said, "This candle represents my dad. He was a great dad and a wonderful man and he worked really hard because he was a very busy man. He had to go out of town a lot and was gone a lot because he was a very busy man. But no matter how hard he worked or how busy he was, every Monday afternoon he would take off early from his job and he would be home when I got home from school. We would play catch and throw the ball around or go for a walk or play a game." Then he paused, wiped the tears from his face, and added: "Now I don't have anything to do on my Monday afternoons."

Another child lit his candle in memory of his mom and said, "I'm lighting this candle in memory of my mom. I remember going for long bike rides with my mom and it was a lot of fun. My dad doesn't like to ride bikes."

Thousands of children have participated in the candlelight ceremony over the past twenty-five years and never once has anyone mentioned a material thing when they share their memories of the person who died. Never has a child said that they remember a new bike or Cabbage Patch kid or video game or anything that a parent *bought* them.

Instead, they remember who we were, what we smelled like, the perfume or cologne we wore. They tell of bike riding, playing ball, baking cookies, getting to stay up late at their grandparent's house and watching movies, etc. They talk about going fishing with Grandpa, or going to Grandma's house for Thanksgiving and smelling the pies cooling on the back porch as they got out of the car and ran to the door.

When we die, what our children cherish most is the time we spent with them and the things we did with them. Please don't spend so much time *buying* them material things. Build memories, instead.

Stephanie and Austin lighting their candles

Follow-Up Support

When Camp Amanda ends and the families return home, they do not expect to hear from Amanda the Panda again, but that is not the case. Since the children want to see each other again and they cannot return to camp unless a subsequent death occurs, they are invited, instead, to come to Amanda the Panda *fun days*, opportunities to just come and play again. Sometimes, they are invited to a water park and pizza party. Other times, it might be a picnic, bowling, a Halloween party, or other event. Always, everyone is invited to the annual Christmas party.

Camp Amanda families do not generally attend Christmas parties; their hearts are so heavy at that time of year that they would rather skip the holidays altogether and jump from October to January. However, they will travel miles to come to Amanda the Panda's Christmas party because they know that it will be a safe place where they will be with friends again.

Holiday Cheer Boxes

Another project that comes as a total surprise to them is a Holiday Cheer Box. Each year, selected families are targeted to receive a cheer box from Amanda the Panda. Usually the boxes are sent to Camp Amanda families who are facing their first holidays following a death in their family.

Each October, decorated Amanda the Panda Holiday Cheer Boxes are placed in the community for three weeks. The empty boxes are delivered to local businesses, churches, and schools who wish to participate. Their employees, congregations, and students fill the boxes to overflowing with new items from the list of suggested items attached to the empty boxes. At the end of three weeks, the filled boxes are returned to Amanda the Panda. The boxes are emptied, and the contents are sorted by categories and placed on tables.

All the toys for girls are on one side of the room and the toys for boys are on the other. Teen gifts and adult gifts are also sorted, along with stuffed animals, jigsaw puzzles, board games, cookbooks, calendars, family videos, microwave popcorn, flavored coffees and teas, journals, *Chicken Soup for The Soul* books, pen and pencil sets, boxed stationery, etc.

Once all the items are sorted, the empty boxes are filled with twenty-five gifts specifically chosen for the families who will receive them, based on the age and gender of everyone living in the home. Each day, a different member of the family opens that day's gift.

Volunteers seem to magically appear to wrap all the gifts and put a sticker on each one that says, "Open Me December 1," "Open Me December 2," etc. Thousands of gifts are wrapped each year.

Inside each box is also a letter which says, "We know the holidays will be hard for you this year and we want you to know that someone is thinking of you." The boxes are a total surprise and arrive at their destinations just in time for their first gift to be opened on the first of December. Since 1993 when this project first began, 30,525 gifts have been donated or purchased, selected, gift-wrapped, and sent to 1221 families!

Margaret with just a few of the many items placed in Holiday Cheer boxes

Ashlin and Makayla

Chapter 11

Canine Companions
Four-Legged Healers

One day, a camp application from an eight-year-old boy came across JoAnn's desk. His name was Cody and his mother had recently died by suicide. Shortly thereafter, his three dogs also died by eating contaminated dog food! What a heavy burden for a little boy to carry - the death of his mother *and* his three dogs, too!

As she read his application and looked at his photo, JoAnn's heart was deeply moved. She was determined to have a dog at camp for Cody, but it would have to be very well-mannered and well-trained. It would have to be gentle and loving and be the kind of dog that a boy like Cody could snuggle with and confide in - a dog that would provide unconditional love. It would have to be one that would love him and even be willing to lick away his tears. At the very least, Cody and all the children at camp deserved to have a four-legged healer by their sides.

As JoAnn began to research organizations that train dogs, a friend suggested she contact Canine Companions for Independence (CCI), a national organization that breeds, trains, and provides highly trained assistance dogs for people with disabilities. Some of the dogs become "facility dogs" and are assigned to various non-profit organizations that serve children or adults. Facility dogs receive the same training as service dogs and must pass the same exams to graduate.

JoAnn applied to CCI and was paired with the perfect dog for such a special mission - a golden retriever named Sela. JoAnn and Sela went through team training together and graduated as a team just in time for the camp which Cody was scheduled to attend.

Team training was an intense two-week period of classes in which the participants learned all about dogs - their health, dispositions, grooming and teeth brushing, how dogs think, how to encourage and correct them, and finally, how to be their leader.

Each morning was spent in classes, and each afternoon was spent working with the dogs and becoming a team together. At night, there were take-home tests for another hour and a half. It was an exhausting two weeks of training to learn what the dogs already knew – over fifty commands.

The second week was an opportunity to put into action what had been learned in the classroom with field trips to various locations in the city, including the malls, the zoo, a restaurant, a pet store, and a trip to Wal-Mart. The dogs were always on their best behavior, and the teams were constantly being watched and evaluated. There were several commands that had to be demonstrated in action, such as purchasing a small item like a greeting card and having the dog *pay* the cashier. The dog would *get* a credit card that had been intentionally dropped on the floor, *hold* it in its mouth as the handler said, "*Let's go*", leading the dog to the counter. The dog would then put its paws *up* on the counter and *give* the credit card to the cashier. When the cashier had completed her transaction, the dog would *get* the purchased greeting card, get *off* the counter, and *give* it to the handler.

The teams performed flawlessly. In addition to all the field trip tests, there was a final written exam over all the material that had been covered during the two weeks of training. After passing the exam, the teams were allowed to graduate and take the dogs home to begin the work they would ultimately do.

All CCI dogs spend the first year of their lives with volunteer puppy raisers who agree to keep the dogs for one year, giving them the best start a puppy could have. In that first year, puppy raisers take their dogs to puppy school and dog obedience school, as well as teach them twenty-two commands. They also socialize the dogs to many different life experiences, such as taking them to work, the grocery store, the movies, doctor's appointments, church, airplane rides, restaurants, etc. At the end of their first year, they return the dogs to CCI for advanced training where they learn the skills needed to open and close doors, turn lights on and off, pick things up off the floor, and pay by credit card.

At the graduation ceremony, the dogs are reunited with their puppy raisers for a short time and they sit in the audience with them. At the appropriate time in the ceremony, the puppy raiser turns over the leash and the dog to the graduate. It is a true labor of love on the part of all the volunteer puppy raisers! A very special thank you to Sela's volunteer puppy raiser, Ann Schenkel, who did an outstanding job of raising her and being her human "mom" for her first year of life.

There are not enough good things to say about CCI and all the dedicated, competent, professional, and loving trainers, volunteer puppy raisers, and breeders/caretakers that make up this awesome organization. They are absolutely the best! For more information on CCI, visit their website at www.caninecompanions.org

When Cody arrived at Camp Amanda and saw Sela, his face lit up. It is a picture permanently etched in JoAnn's mind and heart. Cody spotted Sela as soon as he came to register for camp. He was instantly attracted to her the moment he first saw her, and his face absolutely beamed! He and Sela became instant friends who were nearly inseparable the entire weekend. Sela gave Cody lots of wet kisses, and Cody threw his arms around Sela. The two of them just loved each other. Sela has never met a child whom she has not loved instantly. She is a natural around all children, and the more the merrier. She is so very gentle and loving. She has become known as the "gentle giant."

Sela was retired early as a facility dog for medical reasons, but she continues to visit the children at each camp, giving them her boundless love and allowing them to walk her. She cannot run and play hard with them, but she can and does love them well. Sela lives with her best friend, Ashlin, and JoAnn. Ashlin, also a golden retriever, is JoAnn's successor dog.

Cody (above) and Meghan (below) with Sela at Camp Amanda

Best Friends — Sela and Ashlin

Ashlin In Reading Class

One of the activities that Ashlin excels at is school visits. Each Wednesday afternoon, Ashlin and JoAnn visit Mrs. Hanasz's third grade class at King Elementary School in Des Moines, Iowa. They visit during reading class.

Each week, Mrs. Hanasz selects the children who will read to Ashlin. Some are selected because they have read beyond what is required of them; some are selected because they have shown the greatest improvement during the week; others are selected because they are not quite reading at the third-grade level yet.

The children really look forward to Wednesdays and Ashlin's visits. Even children who are now in the fifth grade will stop by Mrs. Hanasz's class on Wednesday afternoons just to see Ashlin.

One little boy named Ernie, who is now a fifth grader, always has a smile when he sees Ashlin. When Ernie was in the third grade, he did not enjoy reading because he didn't know how; he was reading at the first-grade level. He told his teacher that he didn't want to read out loud in front of the class because he didn't know all the words. He was embarrassed.

Each week, Ernie would select two or three books to read to Ashlin. He would take her leash and lead her into another room where there was a little couch for two. No one else was in the room but Ernie, Ashlin, and JoAnn. Ernie would sit down and Ashlin would jump up on the couch, sit beside Ernie and put her head in his lap. At first Ernie would begin to read very slowly, often stopping to sound out the words he didn't know. Sometimes, he got them right; sometimes, he didn't. Ashlin didn't mind. She never corrected him or showed any disappointment in him. Sometimes, it even appeared that she was following along.

Ashlin giving a reader a "kiss"

As Ernie reads his favorite book, Ashlin appears to be following along

Week after week, Ernie read to Ashlin. Soon he began to smile more. He seemed much happier. Then he began to comb and style his hair. He took pride in his appearance. There was a certain confidence in him that wasn't there at the beginning of the school year. By late January, he was reading at the third-grade level! One day he even told his teacher that he wanted to read out loud to the class!

Ashlin is Ernie's very special friend. Whenever he sees her, whether he is on the playground or in school, he comes running toward her with a beautiful smile and a confidence about him. Hugs, wet dog kisses, and a wagging tail let him know that Ashlin is very proud of him.

To see more photos of Sela and Ashlin, visit Amanda the Panda's website at: www.amandathepanda.org

Sela enjoys a hug from Megan at camp

Chapter 12
Lessons I Have Learned From Grieving Families

Camp Amanda is the first and longest-running camp for grieving children and families in the country. There are now four other states that have modeled Camp Amanda: Camp Paz in Arizona, Camp Amanda in Washington, Camp Hope in Wisconsin, and Camp Amanda in Minnesota. There are many other states that do not have camps for people grieving a death in their families. Hopefully, that will change soon.

Today, 95% of Amanda's work is with grieving children and families. In 1980 when Amanda was first created, there was very little being done for children living with cancer. That is not the case now.

Today, hospitals have an inter-disciplinary team approach that meets the physical, spiritual, and emotional needs of children with cancer and their families. Many other wonderful organizations also focus on children living with cancer and ways to make their lives much richer and fuller.

Today, grieving individuals are where cancer patients were twenty-five years ago, with little support and services geared toward them. A major difference is they do not have the outward physical signs of the inward pain and suffering they are experiencing. It is easier to identify a child with no hair or one who is missing a limb than it is to identify the pain of a child whose mother or father has died, or the co-worker who finds it hard to concentrate because he or she has recently experienced the death of a spouse or a child.

Death Means Changes
Oftentimes, a death in the family means many other changes as well. It might be a change from living in the country to living in the city, or vice-versa. The death of a single parent might mean the child or children will now be raised by a grandparent or other

relatives or friends or even strangers.

A major move also means the loss of the familiar, replaced instead with a new house, new neighborhood, new school, new teachers, new friends, new job, new expectations. This also means missing old friends, teachers, co-workers, family, and all that is familiar.

A New "Normal"

The old "normal" is gone forever to be replaced by a new normal that is so new, it is hard to call it normal. Every day brings a multitude of adjustments for *every* member of the family. Unfortunately, for those who are bereaved, society is not too accommodating to the time it takes to mourn the death and all the losses associated with the death. Every member of the family experiences his or her own set of losses following a death; while there are similarities, no two people grieve in the same way.

Grief Follows Its Own Calendar

Oftentimes, because of their own discomfort, people place an impossible and misguided expectation on those who are grieving. They think they should "get over it" and be back to "normal" in at least six months! The reality is that no one gets over it, they just learn to get through it, and it *always* takes longer than a few months! Grief is a very individual thing and does not follow a calendar. It takes time, *lots* of it, and the best thing to do is to be patient with others and love them unconditionally, however long it takes.

It takes a year just to get through all the "firsts": first birthday, anniversary, Mother's Day, Father's Day, first holidays. People brace themselves for this year of firsts.

The second year following a death is sometimes more surprising than the first. They knew the first year would be difficult, but the second year seems to take them by surprise. They expected it to be easier somehow. Instead, the full reality of what it means to be without their loved one is inescapable. Some say the second year is harder in many ways.

Grieving people frequently share that it is not until the *third* year that they begin to feel like they have the energy and desire to plug back into activities that they once enjoyed.

The Missing Pieces Of The Puzzle

Grieving families want people to know that it is important for friends and relatives to mention their loved one's name and to share their personal memories with them. One mother described her deceased child as a *puzzle* with many *missing pieces*. Unless friends shared their stories of her son and the things they did together when he was with them, her puzzle would never be complete. She needed their pieces! She wanted to hear all the funny things her son did when she was not with him: things that made him laugh, times he might have gotten in trouble.

Stories are precious, especially when they are about a person who is no longer living. All that the survivors have left are memories, and they hunger to hear their loved one's name mentioned by family and friends and to hear other people's stories.

Children Are Our Greatest Teachers

The most valuable lesson I have learned in working with children with life-threatening illnesses is that *today* is very important. Yesterday is over, and tomorrow may or may not come. Today is a gift to be treasured.

When I would come home after a day of visiting the children, I couldn't wait to hug my own kids. It is such a gift to have children who are healthy. It is nothing we earn or even deserve. It is pure gift.

The most important lesson I have learned from my work is to tell people that you love them *today*, while you still can. There is no guarantee that they - or you - will be here tomorrow. If someone has hurt you or you have hurt them, make peace *today*. Don't delay, you may never have another chance to make things right.

Live With No Regrets

If you have been meaning to write a letter or e-mail someone, do it today. If you intended to call a friend or relative and haven't had the time, do it now. Bake cookies with your children today. Ride bikes together, play with them; make memories while you can.

Don't put things off until you have more time; you may not. Hug someone today and tell the people you live with that you love them. People whose loved ones have died would give anything to have one more day with them – just to be able to say or do the things they never had a chance to. We still have that chance – *today*.

Amanda and the children send you a big bear hug

Epilogue
The Next Chapter Waiting To Be Written

It seems that with every step of the twenty-five year journey that I have been on, God has directed my path. There is no doubt in my mind that this is God's work and these are His children. I am merely one who listens to His voice and says, "I will go, Lord, if you lead me. I will hold your people in my heart."

Sometimes, that's a scary thing to say to God or to anyone else because you never know exactly where it will lead you. I have given many talks to various groups over the years, locally, nationally, and even internationally, and repeatedly, people have said, "You have so many stories to tell, you should write a book."

I am not a writer. I have never before written a book. I appeased the voices that were compelling me to write by answering, "Someday, when I have the time, I may." But I didn't really think it would happen.

Then, this year I heard God saying to me, "This is the year. This is the 'someday' you have been talking about. It is time. The children's stories need to be told, and I want you to write them down from your heart."

I am beginning to believe that the writing of this book is intimately connected with the next chapter of the life of Amanda the Panda – which involves serving many more children and families.

An Invitation

I believe that everyone who reads this book is being given an invitation to be a part of it. I don't know how, but the how doesn't really matter; it is not for me to figure out.

It is for you to search your heart and to listen. The rest will be revealed. It is not by accident that you have purchased or received this book and read these stories; it is by *design* and for a *purpose*.

Sometimes, I feel like the "old woman in the shoe" who has so many children she doesn't know what to do. There are children on waiting lists for all of our services, including camps, support groups, and fun days.

In the past, there have been four Camp Amanda weekends each year for grieving children and families, yet people were put on waiting lists for months at a time. Due to space restrictions at the camp we rent, Camp Amanda has been limited to just two camps per year for the past four years, in May and September. These are the least desirable months of the year because children are simply not available.

The month of May is already jam-packed with other activities, such as the end of the school year and the beginning of Little League, soccer, Mother's Day, graduations, family weddings, reunions, and so much more.

The month of September is less than ideal for a variety of other reasons. It is the beginning of the school year, which means that teachers and school counselors, who are the major source of referral to camp, are just beginning to know their students and may not be aware of the deaths that have occurred in families. Also, the beginning of the school year means the start of a variety of organized and extra-curricular school and sports activities that involve children.

At present, Amanda the Panda does not own camp property. Instead, for more than fifteen years space has been rented from an existing church camp in central Iowa. It is an ideal location because it is the only camp with facilities that accommodate two completely distinct camps – the children's camp and the adult's camp – to be held simultaneously, but separately.

Although there are many other existing campsites in Iowa, all of them share the same dining hall and kitchen, which means that the children and their parents will inevitably be in the same location at the same time. When this occurs, young children become homesick for their parents, and neither of them gets the full benefit of a camp exclusively for them.

An Incredible Offer

A few months ago, a gentleman from Minnesota called me and said he had heard of Camp Amanda and wanted to donate his land if we would bring the children to Minnesota for camp. He told me that his only daughter was killed years ago in an accident, and his only brother had also died.

He said, "My parents and I own forty acres of land with a pond on it and lots of trees. We have farmed the land all of our lives. Now we are retired. We took the old farmhouse and made a duplex out of it, and my parents, who are in their eighties, live on one side while my wife and I, who are in our sixties, live on the other side. There is no future generation to leave the land to when we die. We would like to leave a legacy and we can't think of anything we would like better than to have children on the land. We wondered if it would be suitable for your camp?"

I nearly fell out of my chair! If only he and his land were in IOWA! I believe that God speaks directly to us *and* through others, as well as through beauty and nature. When children light their candles at Camp Amanda and share memories of their loved ones who died, it is truly *holy* ground. The word that best describes the candlelight ceremony is *sacred*.

I think the Minnesota farmer understood that and knew that we would honor his land by using it to heal children's broken hearts. He could envision it being filled with children running, playing, laughing, singing, and even fishing from his pond. It appealed to him to know that his land would be the place where children would be healers for one another.

Support Groups

Currently, support groups for grieving families are offered every other Tuesday from 6:00 - 7:30 P.M. A simple meal is served, and then everyone goes to their respective, age-appropriate group. Every available office and hallway space is utilized. Since we have no kitchen or dining hall, volunteers prepare the meals at home, bring them to the office, and serve them from tables set up in the reception area, cafeteria-style. Children eat on the floor on plastic tablecloths, while their parents balance their meals on their knees.

There is no place for arts and crafts or expressive play therapy. If the children are noisy, they are heard in the offices where other groups are meeting. There is nowhere for them to play, except in the parking lot! Our space is filled to capacity and cannot accommodate one more child or adult; there is simply no more room.

Is It A Dream Or Is God Speaking?

Could it be that it is time to have an Amanda the Panda Family Grief Center of our own on a few acres of land where day camps could be offered to augment weekend camps in the summer months when children are least busy and most available, as well as during the school year? Where families could come throughout the year for support groups and be able to eat their meals while sitting at tables in a dining room instead of on the floor? Where children can release some of their grief energy outdoors? Where there would be a quiet and peaceful area for a memory garden with flowers, a little brook, benches to sit on, and maybe even a tiny chapel nearby that would accommodate a maximum of thirty people? Where we could have campfires and roast hot dogs and have s'mores? Where we could have camper reunions? Where everything – camp supplies, support group supplies, office supplies, and cheer box gifts - would be under one roof instead of at five separate off-site locations, as is the case now? Where we could have Amanda the Panda fun days and invite entire families to come and play? Where we could offer training for people in other states to come and learn how they can put on a camp for grieving children in their area? Where educational seminars could be offered to educators, mental health professionals, nurses, and funeral directors? Where a panel of children could teach them what is helpful and what is not helpful in the grieving process? Where parts of the facility could be rented out, when available, for corporate retreats, family reunions, and various types of workshops?

More Desirable, Less Costly

Actually, an Amanda the Panda *Family Grief Center* on a few acres of land in the city is more desirable and less expensive to maintain than a camp of our own on forty acres of land.

Is this a dream, or is this the direction the Lord is leading me? If it is a dream, it keeps recurring. If it is from the Lord, then I have only one thing to say, *"Here I am, Lord. Is it I, Lord? I have heard you calling in the night. I will go, Lord, if you lead me. I will hold your people in my heart."*

I hear you, Lord! But it would cost millions of dollars to build such a facility, and it would have to be located in the city to accommodate the urban population who attend our support groups. Land in the city or western suburbs is exorbitantly expensive! Lord, you know that I have no money. Are you *really* leading me in this direction? It seems a gigantic and impossible task!

I heard Him say, "Where is your faith? Do you really believe in Me? Then trust in Me and let the children come to me!"

Perhaps You Are A Part Of The Next Chapter

I don't know how this will all come to be. Perhaps there is a developer who has land in the city that would be perfect for a family grief center and, like my Minnesota farmer, would like to donate it to Amanda the Panda and leave a legacy of his own. Perhaps school children across America would like to save their pennies, nickels, dimes, and quarters to help other children whose parent or sibling has died. Perhaps there are people with money, either yourself or someone you know, who want to leave a legacy and are looking for a worthy cause to donate it to.

Perhaps you have some ideas. If so, please write to me. I do know that it will take a lot of people to make it happen: children, teens, and adults who believe that if we join forces and work together, anything is possible.

Nothing Is Impossible With God

We would need *everything*: prayers, land, money, supplies, furniture, workers, dreamers, builders and planners, architects, constructions workers. It would truly take a whole army of people working together to make it happen and a whole lot of money. It sure seems impossible from where I stand now. At the same time, I know that nothing is impossible with God.

For the past twenty-five years, we have never charged a family a penny for Amanda the Panda's services. God has always provided. We have never had a lot of money, but we have always had enough. Isn't that all that anyone really needs?

In the early years of Amanda the Panda, my husband worked two jobs to "support my *Amanda* habit." He is a high school math teacher by day and taught at Drake University at night so that I could quit my job at the savings and loan and devote myself fulltime to be Amanda the Panda. It was a volunteer position for many years and only became a salaried position when our children were approaching college age.

I truly do not know where God is leading. I do know that if this is the direction he wants me to take, I will go.

Is He calling you, too? *Together*, we can make it happen. I believe that. *Together* and with one voice we can say, *"Here I am, Lord. Is it I, Lord? I have heard you calling in the night. I will go, Lord, if you lead me. I will hold your people in my heart."*

JoAnn Zimmerman

About the Author

JoAnn Zimmerman is the creator of Amanda the Panda and founder of Amanda Cares, Inc., a non-profit organization under which all Amanda the Panda programs operate.

During the past twenty-five years, her work has been featured in *Life Magazine, Better Homes and Gardens, Catholic Digest, Family Circle,* and *Bereavement magazine.*

She has appeared on *Good Morning America* and has been a presenter to national and international conferences such as the *World Gathering on Bereavement,* the *International Conference on Children and Death,* and the *National Hospice Organization.*

JoAnn is a wife, mother, and proud grandmother of four. She lives in Des Moines, Iowa with her husband of thirty-eight years, Joe, and her two golden retrievers, Sela and Ashlin.

JoAnn writes and speaks "from the heart." The stories in this book were forever wrapped around her heart as she lived them, and now have spilled over into a book written simply and beautifully that will touch your heart.

Mom's Letter

I print this letter from my mother out of a deep love and respect for her. She simply did not understand my "calling" to be a bear. Sometimes, one has to listen to the voice within and do what they feel God is calling them to do, despite outside opposition. I waited for several months before I told her that I had quit my job to be a bear. Below is her priceless response. Enjoy.

Crotone, Italy   March 21, 1981
My dear and beloved daughter,

The day after I spoke with you by phone, I received your letter telling me about Amanda the Panda. I would have written sooner, but I had to cool off a little.

Yes, my precious daughter, what you are doing is sublime and very Christian. Beautiful. Wonderful. But God had you assigned for a different mission. Had you assigned to one of the best mission of all. The mission of wife and <u>mother</u>. That's your mission which require a <u>full-time job</u>.

You can't help other people's children and leave your own in strange hands plus you got to pay for a babysitter and yet the children are living in and out of the yard, eating out of the refrigerator or out of the cookie jar because mom don't have the time to cook for them a hot lunch or a nice dinner.

Most of all, the children need their mother's comfort. I repeat, what you are doing is good, but that's a job for single people, for people that don't have other responsibilities and they can dedicate themselves for others.

Naturally you are bringing to others lots of comfort but in the same time you are doing lots of harm to you and to your family, financially

133

and morally.

And another thing, your name is JoAnn – that's the name we give to our daughter and they better don't change the beautiful name with the B.S. Amanda, whoever it is.

Well, anyway, hope the good Lord will illuminate you.

Forever Your mother

P.S. Go back to work.

I'll Lend You A Child

I'll lend you for a little time,
A child of mine, God said,
For you to love the while she lives
And mourn for when she's dead.

It may be six or seven weeks
Or thirty years, or three
But will you, till I call her back
Take good care of her for me?

She'll bring her charm to gladden you
And should her stay be brief
You'll have her lovely memories
As solace for your grief.

I cannot promise she will stay
Since all from earth return,
But there are lessons taught down there
I want this child to learn.

I looked the wide world over
In my search for teachers true,
And from the throngs who crowd life's way
I selected you.

Now will you give her all your love
Nor think the labor vain
Nor hate me when I call around
To take her back again?

I fancy that I hear you say
Dear Lord, Thy will be done
For all the joy this little child has brought
All fateful risks we run.

We sheltered her with tenderness
We loved her while we may
And for the happiness we've known
We shall forever grateful stay.

But you came round to call for her
Much sooner than we planned
Dear Lord, forgive this grief
And help us understand.

The following grief story is reprinted with permission from Grief Digest, *Centering Corporation, Omaha, Nebraska, (402) 553-1200*

The Girl in the Porcelain Bowl

A long time ago, in ancient China, there lived an older couple who had a beautiful daughter. As the daughter reached womanhood, the father died. The mother and daughter mourned, and shortly after the father's death, the mother herself grew sick – sick unto death. Before she died, she called her daughter to her.

"My child," she said. "You are very beautiful. I do not want someone to marry you just for your beauty alone."

And with that, she placed over the girl's head a beautiful porcelain bowl. The bowl changed colors with the sunlight. It shone and shimmered when the girl moved. And all you could see of the girl in the porcelain bowl was her mouth and chin. Then the mother died.

The girl, being very poor, went to work in the rice fields belonging to a rich farmer. She worked hard and made many friends. In a very short time, her friends gathered around her and said, "Let us help you get that bowl off your head."

They pulled. They pounded. They twisted, but the bowl would not budge. All that happened was that the girl woke up the next morning with a really bad headache!

The wealthy farmer noticed the girl in the porcelain bowl. He saw how she treated other workers, the grace with which she moved, her manner and demeanor, and he saw how hard she worked. One day he approached the girl in the porcelain bowl and asked her to come with him, live in his home and care for his wife, who was ill.

From the first day the girl in the porcelain bowl moved into the big house owned by the farmer, she was loved. The farmer and his wife thought of her as their own child. She cared diligently for the wife, and she made friends with the other servants. One day her friends gathered around her and said, "Let us help you get that bowl off your head."

They pulled. They pounded. They twisted, but the bowl would not budge. All that happened was the girl woke up the next morning with a really bad headache!

141

One day, the young son of the farmer came home from studying abroad. He saw the girl in the porcelain bowl. He saw how she cared for his mother. He saw how she had the respect of everyone in his house. He asked her to go for a walk with him. They walked and talked many times, and in a very short time the farmer's son had fallen in love with the girl in the porcelain bowl and he asked her to marry him.

"I cannot marry you," she said. "I am but a servant in your father's house."

Over and over he asked, and each time she gave the same reply.

One night the girl in the porcelain bowl cried herself to sleep, for she, too, loved the farmer's son. That night her mother appeared to her in a dream. "My child," the mother said. "I want only happiness for you. Marry the farmer's son."

So the next day, the girl in the porcelain bowl waited for her beloved to ask her to marry him, and when he did, she said, "Yes!"

"Let the feasts begin," the boy shouted, and family and friends came from miles around.

On the night before their wedding, the farmer's son was drinking with his friends from afar when one of the friends said loudly to the farmer's son, "Do you know she has a bowl on her head? She might be really ugly under there. You don't know what is under that bowl." And the girl overheard him.

The next morning she went to her bridegroom. "I cannot marry you!" she said. "I have this bowl on my head!"

The farmer's son took the girl's chin in his hand and kissed her lips. "I love you!" he said, "I love you, bowl or no bowl."

And with that, the most amazing thing happened. The bowl shattered into a million pieces and from it fell gold and silver and precious jewels, and everyone there saw that not only was the girl very beautiful, she was indeed very, very rich.

This is a grief story. When we grieve, it's as if we're covered with a porcelain bowl. We cannot see clearly. People can't see us, either. Over and over friends say, "Let us help you get over this grief," and they tug and pound and we have a terrible headache. We're miserable. But once we realize our loved one who died would want only happiness for us, we can begin to reach out. There will be setbacks, of course, but once we know we are loved, grief or no grief, our sorrow can shatter and people will see that through our grief we have become beautiful, indeed . . . and very, very rich.

BOOK ORDER FORM

To order more copies of **FROM THE HEART OF A BEAR** for yourself or to give as gifts to family and friends:

JoAnn Zimmerman

10516 Meredith Dr. Unit 2

Urbandale, IA 50322

jzpanda@aol.com

eady.

515-988-4116

(Please print)
Please send me _____ copies of your book @ $19.95.
                    Iowa Residents, please add $1.20
Shipping and Handling:
U.S.: $4.00 for first book and $2.00 for each additional.
Int'l: $9.00 for first book; $5.00 for all others (estimate).

( ) Credit Card   ( ) Mastercard   ( ) Visa
Card Number_____ Exp. Date_____

_____
Name on card   Zip code of billing address

Mail to: _____
            First Name   Last Name

_____
Address

_____
City   State   Zip

_____
Daytime Phone with Area Code   Evening Phone

_____
E-mail Address

THANK YOU FOR YOUR ORDER ☺